Channels of Grace

HOW TO SEAMLESSLY CONNECT & STAY CONNECTED WITH GOD

Emmanuel Adewusi

CCCG Publishing House

Contents

Dedication	vii
Preface	ix
Introduction	xi
1 A Case for Grace	1
2 Hindrances to Grace	16
3 Channels of Grace	25
4 Impartation of Grace	73
5 Evidence of Connection	115
Epilogue	121
Contact the Author	127
A Sinner's Prayer	129
About The Author	130

Copyright © 2022 Emmanuel Adewusi

All rights reserved. No part of this book may be used or reproduced by any means, graphics, electronic, or mechanical, including photocopying, recording, taping, or by any information storage retrieval system without the author's written permission except in cases of brief quotations embodied in critical articles and reviews.

Scriptures are taken from the New King James Version. Copyright 1979, 1980, 1982 by Thomas Nelson, Inc. Used by permission. All right reserved.

Author: Emmanuel Adewusi

ISBN: 978-1-989099-04-9 (hardcover)
ISBN: 978-1-989099-09-4 (ebook)

First Printing 2022

I am grateful to my Heavenly Father, Jesus Christ, and the person of the Holy Spirit for the ability to receive and complete this very important assignment. Contribution to mankind's advancement is not something I take for granted.

I also owe gratitude to my book writing team for their time and effort in meticulously editing this work. May God bless you all.

To my lovely wife, Ibukun Adewusi, thank you for always being dependable, reliable, and selfless in ensuring that kingdom work is done with excellence.

To everyone looking to grow in their ability to connect with the King of kings and the Lord of lords, I pray that this book will enhance your efforts.

Preface

I don't know about you, but in the past, I have gotten to points where I've said, "you know what? I can't do this anymore. I'm done!" If you've gotten to this point before, know that this is a cry for more grace! Paul said, *"Therefore I take pleasure in infirmities, in reproaches, in needs, in persecutions, in distresses, for Christ's sake. For when I am weak, then I am strong"* (2 Corinthians 12:10). Apostle Paul acknowledged while at his wit's end that he needed grace.

It took me a while to realize that the grace of God seeks to empower those who are weak, not those who are strong. Grace is a free and unmerited virtue that we receive from God. It helps us do things that we are otherwise unable to do, and the more we understand this, our growth in grace will increase. According to 2 Chronicles 16:9, the eyes of the Lord are going to and fro to show Himself strong to those who are weak. It means that the grace of God will always skip a strong person to rest upon a weak person.

That is why the Bible says that the kingdom of heaven belongs to those who are poor in spirit. *"Blessed are the poor in spirit: for theirs is the kingdom of heaven"* (Matthew 5:3). The poor in spirit are those who allow themselves to be brought to the point of weakness where they acknowledge that while they might have some strength, compared to God, they have nothing. We must constantly be in that state of mind. The grace of God will never empower a strong person. It is only made available to those who are weak.

I wrote this book to assist those genuine God-chasers who are seeking a faster and deeper connection with God. I encourage you to read this book with an open heart to enable it to correct, strengthen and instruct you in righteousness.

Introduction

You'll see something very interesting when studying the New Testament, especially throughout the book of Acts. The Bible illustrates how the Holy Spirit filled the people and empowered the Apostles. But what does this mean? It means that prior to the outpouring of the Holy Ghost, they were empty vessels. In essence, they approached God in humility as weak vessels but left the presence of God filled with grace that made them strong. Remember that the Bible says that God resists the proud but gives grace to the humble (James 4:6).

For many of us, it is when we are at our wit's end and genuinely know that there is no other way out that we receive help from God. However, when everything is fine, we pray casually and consequently don't receive visitations or answers from God. Several scriptures confirm that God responds when His children cry to Him (Judges 3:9, Judges 4:3, Judges 6:7). The mere fact that the Word of God uses "cry" means that we must position ourselves to act like a baby because babies cry because of their dependency on others for their basic needs. When we approach God like a little child, divine visitations will become a regular occurrence.

We'll never see the perfection of grace until there is "weakness or until we assume a childlike posture." Someone said there is a reason we are all called children of God and not adults of God. Therefore, no matter how old you are or how many children you have, you'll realize that when you come to God, you must come like a baby; otherwise, you may not receive anything. Like a child, come to God without assumptions. Understand and reassure yourself that you're meeting with the Creator of the heavens and earth. One of the ways you can do this is by approaching God's throne with an attitude of gratitude instead of a mindset of entitlement. It's a privilege to be able to approach the King of kings, especially when we acknowledge that we are only human beings and have failings.

It's comforting to rest in the fact that the grace of God is available in seasons where it seems as though you have been gifted with what Paul called "a thorn in the flesh." Paul cried out to God, the way many of us have in one season or another, for God to remove our suffering. But God being so loving, gave us this wonderful survival kit called sufficient grace. If we're genuine with ourselves, many would admit that if not for the "thorn in their flesh," the challenges or the opposition, they would not be as grounded in Christ as they are now. Why? Because they've realized their inherent weakness and deep need for grace.

Grace does not equate to the absence of problems. Instead, it is the ability to deal with difficulties easily and, in some cases, even without stress. There will be times when God may not take problems we face away, but he will give us the grace to get through the situation. But regardless of the thorns, grace allows us to do way more than people who didn't have thorns in their flesh. Think of it like this - both a sedan and a cylindrical truck may have to move the same load. While the load may be the same, the truck will fare much better because the engine is different. Similarly, we may face the same difficulties as another person, but our capacity to navigate through that same problem is much higher because of our engine, also known as grace.

In Exodus 4, we are told how Moses refused to answer God's call on his life because of the insecurity he had with his speech. After going back and forth with God, Moses finally took on the call to rescue the Israelites. The amazing thing about this story is that God never removed the stammer but instead supplied him with grace. Despite the stammering, he still fulfilled the assignment that God called him to do. In the Old Testament, instructions were given and had to be carried out purely by strength. However, in the New Testament era that we are currently in, while God is still giving us instructions, He has now supplied us with the grace to follow them. The arm of flesh will fail, and according to 1 Samuel 2:9, *"for by strength, no man shall prevail."* No man can continuously obey God in the flesh; It is impossible. If we are now walking by grace, then we are walking in the flesh.

What does it mean to be walking in the flesh? Anything void of the Holy Ghost is akin to walking in the flesh. We're often given divine instructions and think that we can carry them out on our own. You'll know you're walking in the flesh when you're deliberately not asking for help. That is why I say that prayerlessness is pride. Many people still find this difficult to understand, but the absence of prayer and asking for help is pretty much you saying, "I can do this on my own." No one in their right mind would continue to drive a car when the gas tank shows empty. We have all been taught that a car will not run without gas. And similarly, this is what help from God is like.

If you see yourself achieving results beyond the resources you've invested in a particular area, then know that the strength you've generated to carry out that task is not coming from the flesh but purely from God; and that my friend is grace! If everything you do is within your capacity, then either grace is not there, or it is extremely low. But when we can look back and marvel at how we were able to accomplish so much, then we know without a shadow of a doubt that the grace of God was made available and that He was indeed running that race with us.

When we can function beyond our natural capacity and still have the ability to move forward where others would have broken down, we know that there was a force propelling us forward. That is grace at work. We are not designed to function in our own strength, especially when doing spiritual things. Spiritual things are not designed to be done with natural strength. This is why you cannot effectively pray for an hour in your strength. It is all by the grace of God. You can scroll through social media for at least 2 or 3 hours and not fall asleep, but the moment you pick up the Bible and read in your strength, you'll suddenly think, "I never knew I was this sleepy."

That's why Apostle Paul said in Acts 26:22, *"having obtained help from God to this day I stand."* When dealing with that problematic employee, colleague, friend, or family member that you cannot handle on your own, call on God for grace to cohabit with that person and not lose your mind. You are losing your mind because you are devoid of grace. When grace is there, you'll be able to love beyond your natural ability. When you think about Jesus on the cross, and even while in pain, He could say, *"Father, forgive them, for they do not know what they do"* (Luke 23:34). We know that grace was at work because no human being can do that in their strength while in pain. The Bible aptly says, *For the law was given through Moses, but grace and truth came through Jesus* (John 1:17). Jesus Christ came to make grace readily available to every child of God. May you receive grace as you read this book in Jesus' name.

1

A Case for Grace

People struggle when there is no grace. It's not the work they've been given but rather the lack of grace. The Bible tells us about Josiah who was enthroned as king at the age of eight and was ruling one of the most stubborn and stiff-necked groups of people (2 Chronicles 34). Can you imagine how much grace was required to undertake this task successfully and without stress?

When there is grace, you will laugh at the same things that were once the source of your stress! If you're stressed, God will not give you more responsibility but will take away from what you already have because He is not a giver of stress nor its cause. But know that there is beauty in responsibility. The more the responsibility, the more the blessing.

God is not mocked. Whatsoever a man sows, that shall he reap. God created us to do many things, but also to work. If you read Genesis 3, you will notice that the Bible says that when God made everything, no rain had fallen on the earth yet. Why? Because there was no man there to till the ground. That was why He was causing mist from the ground to water the vegetation.

When God made Adam, He didn't tell him, "Just chill, the angels will come to feed and bathe you." No! He said, "tend the garden." Today, you find Christians that don't want to do anything. They say: "Lord, lift this from me."; "put the food in my mouth."; "remove my clothes."; "remove my shoes." God wants us to work, and He can give us the grace to do it without stress. You hear Christians now saying, "Thank God it's Friday!" I thank God for every day, including Monday! There is dignity in work, and we need divine grace to carry out that work with poise.

John 1:17 brings us into the New Testament era of grace, *For the law was given through Moses, but grace and truth came through Jesus Christ.* Meaning that Jesus' death on the cross freed Christians from the requirement of keeping the law. Since His death fulfilled the law and paid the price, we are not bound by the ten or 600+ commandments. As you continue to read, you'll see why grace is the better and much easier route; but I will mention just a few of the many benefits below.

1. **Grace allows us to do more than those under the law.** Take tithing, for example; someone who is under the law would say, "I must give my 10% to God. I MUST do it." Whereas someone under grace would say, "10% is too little. Because Jesus died on the cross, I will give 90% and take 10%!" Most people would not even think of that, which is why it is grace.
2. **Grace justifies us.** When operating in grace, it is as if we have never sinned. Someone that was a prostitute or a chronic liar is justified and can stand and preach the Word of God without condemnation.
3. **Grace empowers us.** When the grace of God comes upon you, supernatural strength will be released. Apostle Paul made it clear that he was who he was by the grace of God. God's grace on Apostle Paul made him labour more than all the other apostles (1 Corinthians 15:10).

4. **Grace is tangible.** The effect of grace upon a Christian can be seen and felt. Grace is not an abstract concept. The grace of God is energy that can be felt and can produce tangible results. In Zechariah 4:7, we see that the shout of grace can release power for generating tangible results.
5. **Grace allows us to be saved through faith.** The whole essence of grace is that we can now have access to spiritual blessings before paying the price of following the law. In the Old Testament, the Jews had to follow the law to be justified. In this New Testament era, we are justified by the grace we receive when we believe in the finished work of Jesus Christ on the cross.
6. **Grace has many virtues, such as favour, power, strength, wisdom, knowledge, and understanding.**

Understand that in this era of grace, God is committed to giving His children the help they need to obey His instructions in this era of grace. One way to know a person operating under grace is the sequence they follow when they receive an instruction from God. The person operating under grace will wait to receive help from God before they run to obey the instruction they received from the Lord. A person not operating under grace will start running to obey an instruction before receiving grace. I have observed that some people operate without grace because they either do not know they are entitled to grace, or they believe they can operate without grace. Contrarily, those NOT under grace do not believe they can receive a promise and see it come to pass without having to personally do anything. They ask what to do to get the promise and keep doing it until they reach the point where they believe they are worthy enough to receive the promise. Most believe that they must toil and strive until they are worthy enough to receive God's promises. This is a wrong mindset. While there are many promises we cannot receive until the requisite works have been completed, there are dimensions we can attain also based on the work that others have done on our behalf. The grace of God has been made available to you; reach out and receive it. This book will show you the way to every grace you desire from God.

Prerequisites to Accessing God's Grace

A 1st-year university student cannot be granted access to register for 2nd-year courses until they have completed the required number of 1st-year courses. In like manner, before a person operates in the channels of grace, they must meet the prerequisites to gain access. The first requirement is you must be born again, and the second requirement after being born again is to ensure you're not living in sin.

Many of us have water in our faucets. You pay your bill so that water flows out when you turn on the tap. But where does that water come from? There is a source of water where pipes are connected that makes water available to you and me.

Similarly, when we drive a car and see the fuel level is low, we go to the gas station and connect the gas pump to our vehicles, and the gas begins to flow. When we are done filling up our tank, we remove the pump and put it back. The key to the free flow of grace is staying connected continuously to the Holy Spirit.

BECOME BORN AGAIN
If you've never accepted Jesus as your Lord and Savior, you don't have access to the grace of God. Jesus is the door - the Way, the Truth, and the Life! If you're not part of my family and I didn't invite you to my house, but I wake up in the morning and see you lying on my bed, you will see another side of me! Why? Because you have not been invited!

When you give your life to Christ, you now have access to everything Jesus has. Accept Jesus into your heart as your personal Lord and

Savior. You can attend church for many years and even go so far as serving in the house of God, but until you're born again, you're not a child of God. Although my parents are pastors, and I've been in the church since I was young, this did not mean that I was automatically born again. On June 12, 1994, I had to answer the altar call in secondary school.

During one of our Come-and-See events, God gave me more understanding and explained that it is like being in a common-law relationship versus being married. He said most people are in a common-law relationship with Him. They come around, give to Him, and even serve Him, but they are not officially married. While the government might recognize that, God does not, and you can never reap the same benefits reserved for marriage while in a common-law relationship. One of such benefits is the grace of God. If you're reading this book and know that you are currently in a common-law relationship with God yet want to please Him, get married as soon as possible. You don't have to have an elaborate ceremony, simply flip to the end of the book now and recite the prayer to begin your marriage with God. It is easy to please God.

HOLINESS

This can seem like a big word to many, but in a nutshell, it means we must strive to please God. One of the ways we can strive to do this is to ensure that we are not living in sin. There is a difference between falling into sin and living in sin. Our Heavenly Father made provision for the forgiveness of sin because He knows that there is a tendency for us to fall into sin. The Bible tells us in Proverbs 24:16, *For a righteous man may fall seven times, and rise again.* For as many times as you may fall, so long as you are righteous, always get back up as quickly as possible. Romans 6:1 says, *what shall we say then? Shall we continue in sin that grace may abound? Certainly not! How shall we who died to sin live any longer in it?* We cannot continue in sin and expect the grace to keep flowing.

Spiritual experiences are similar, but the channel of grace may not take you to God if you are living in sin. Aaron turned his staff into a snake, and the magicians also did the same, but in the end, Aaron's snake swallowed all Pharaoh's magicians' snakes. Both Aaron and Pharaoh's magicians invoked the supernatural realm for help, but Aaron's supernatural manifestation came from God while that of the magicians came from the devil. When non-Christians meditate, they will be taken to a supernatural realm controlled and manipulated by the devil. On the other hand, when a born-again Christian meditates, they will be in the supernatural realm controlled by the Holy Spirit. We must live a holy life so that we are always assured of our connection with the Holy Spirit when we engage through our channels of grace.

HUMILITY

Almost every culture known to man has a way of identifying humility. Some cultures define humility based on how a person walks, talks, and general appearance. From a biblical perspective, humility simply means to operate in a state of acknowledgement of the hand of God in our lives. A person is humble because they have recognized that they are where they are because of the help they have received from God and man. We must assume the posture of humility for God to lift us up. Some people are so self-absorbed and filled with their egos that they believe they are it all and don't need God, that they have all it takes. They are so full of themselves.

Many people have more faith and belief in the healthcare system and the government than God and often wonder, "why do I need God for anything?" Even religious people may not say that they don't need God with their mouths, but their actions will show that they believe that they don't because it is evident that He is not at the center of their lives.

In short, humility is acknowledging there is a God in control of everything, including the affairs of our lives.

PRAYER

Hebrews 4:16 says, *let us, therefore, come boldly to the throne of grace, that we may obtain mercy and find grace to help in time of need.* Accessing the grace of God can be as simple as talking to God in prayer, saying, "Lord Jesus, I need your grace." If you believe that you can do it on your own, then there's no need to pray, and God will never step into your situation because He is a gentleman who, according to Revelation 3:20, stands at the door and knocks.

Make prayer a priority in your life with the understanding that it is not the number of hours but the quality of prayer that matters. You can pray for ten hours but just be making noise, or you can pray powerfully for 10 minutes. Which of the two do you think is more meaningful and pleasing to God?

REVELATION

This is not just acquiring information, but more so what has gone into your heart as something that you firmly believe. Anytime we gain access to revelation, we multiply in grace. This is confirmed in 2 Peter 1:2, which says, *Grace and peace be multiplied to you in the knowledge of God and of Jesus our Lord.* The more of God you know, the more His grace flows into your life. For instance, some people don't pray about money but have the innate grace for wealth because they have gotten revelation on the law of prosperity and what it takes to acquire wealth.

Now with an understanding of the above and keeping it in mind, every time you come into the house of God, open your heart to receive revelation. Be connected and attentive so revelation can flow into you. "How can we get revelation?" you may ask. Revelation can be obtained by: meditating on the word of God, listening to anointed messages of people who have the fruit of what you want in their lives and reading anointed books.

If most of your time is spent watching shows or scrolling through social media, there is no way you can flow in revelation.

THE HOLY SPIRIT

The Holy Spirit is the powerbase of the believer. The Holy Spirit is not inferior to the Father or Christ but has a different role. Like our Heavenly Father and Jesus Christ, the Holy Spirit was there from the very beginning, hovering over the face of the waters (Genesis 1:2).

Many believers are only believers in the word without the action to match it because they are not filled with the Holy Spirit. It takes the empowerment of the Holy Spirit to serve God.

One of my mentors, who turned 80 years old in 2022, went on a trip with a few younger pastors back in 2015 at the age of 73. They took a private jet and flew to one country, prayed all night, then embarked on a multi-country trip within a matter of days. By the time they returned home, all the younger pastors were talking about how they were so tired and stressed out, although they were not the ones who preached. Meanwhile, my 73-year-old mentor was still strong and ready to go.

Human strength will always lead to stress. Therefore, stress will be inevitable anytime we want to accomplish something solely by human strength. However, when we invite the Holy Spirit into the picture, we'll find ourselves getting things done without stress.

Many things are happening in the spirit that we cannot see, and it would be remiss for us to think that we can face them without the help of the Holy Spirit. I've seen many people trying to do the work of God by strength who either failed or found themselves under immense and unavoidable stress. One day, God opened my wife's eyes and showed her in the spirit how people were firing arrows at me while I was preaching, but the arrows did not touch me. Thankfully I was and still am protected but imagine how detrimental it would be if I were unaware. Therefore, the Bible says, *'Not by might nor by power, but by My Spirit,' says the Lord of hosts.*

I'm not telling you this to scare you, but to help you see the need for a helper. And while there can be many helpers, such as our spouses and spiritual authority, the ultimate helper is the Holy Spirit. The Bible talks about how the wife is a helper. Before I got married, the Holy Spirit told me that there was a level I wouldn't get to without being married. But now, as I look back at some of the things that I've encountered and seen throughout my life, I can without a doubt say, "yes, I really needed a helper."

I was feeding myself as a single man, but even my body could tell the difference after marrying my helper. You might be carrying a particular load, but when the Holy Spirit comes in, He can enable you to carry a heavier load without it looking like you are – this is how you can make an impact. There is way more to life than just eating and working. We are here to make an impact. This is confirmed in Acts 1:8 – *"But you shall receive power when the Holy Spirit has come upon you; and you shall be witnesses to Me in Jerusalem, and in all Judea and Samaria, and to the end of the earth."* This means that when the Holy Spirit comes upon us, it is not for our benefit or to waste casually, but to do God's work and make an impact in His Kingdom.

It should be noted here that there are also demonic spirits that fill people and should never be confused with the Holy Spirit. Many of us might have seen people possessed by demons, acting strangely or erratically. People that are filled with demons are very aggressive, and many of these same people end up saying, "the Holy Spirit made me do it," but it was not actually true. While the devil possesses people and makes them look crazy, the Holy Spirit will never make you do such crazy and foolish things.

Many people that are genuinely filled with the Holy Spirit are the sweetest, gentlest, kindest people you can ever imagine. Always remember that not all shaking and moving is the Holy Spirit; it may just be people looking for attention.

The Holy Spirit gives us power when we allow Him to take charge of our lives. In Acts 1:4, we see that Jesus instructed His disciples to wait for the baptism of the Holy Spirit. Can you imagine the Canadian Military sending their soldiers out for battle without weapons, guns, and gear? That would never happen.

Never attempt to fulfill your destiny without the Holy Spirit. Similarly, God would never allow His children to go into the enemy's territory unprepared. But it is also our job to wait on the Holy Spirit to fill us, give us power, and not prematurely deploy ourselves for war. Many of us go about life doing good without the backing of the Holy Spirit and come back hurt and damaged. This can sometimes give the enemy room to make people believe they were doing the wrong thing or discourage them when they were doing the right things without proper backing. Even Jesus did not start His ministry until He was filled with the Holy Spirit, according to Acts 10:38, which says, *"how God anointed Jesus of Nazareth with the Holy Ghost and with power, who went about doing good, and healing all that were oppressed by the devil, for God was with Him."* The Gospel, according to Luke, was more precise in describing how the anointing of the Holy Spirit came upon Jesus Christ.

When all the people were baptized, it came to pass that Jesus also was baptized; and while He prayed, the heaven was opened. And the Holy Spirit descended in bodily form like a dove upon Him, and a voice came from heaven which said, "You are My beloved Son; in You I am well pleased." (Luke 3:21-22)

Even the apostles followed this same process. Any time people were saved, they ensured that they were also baptized in the Holy Spirit.

Some churches have limited baptism to just water baptism. However, baptism of the Holy Spirit is equally important and necessary as it supplements water baptism to create a synergistic effect that is needed to fulfill our destiny. Some examples of baptism in the Holy Spirit are in Acts 2:38, Acts 8:14-17, and Acts 19:1-6.

Some people may then say, "you know, that's good, but I've already been baptized in the Holy Spirit." But baptism in the Holy Spirit is not just an isolated, one-time occurrence. When we look at Acts 2:1-6, we'll see that the apostles were filled with the Holy Spirit. Yet still, when read further, we'll also see that in Acts 4:43, they were filled again with the Holy Spirit. So, know that even after receiving this baptism, there may be times in your walk when it may be necessary for you to be baptized again and again because of the nature of your calling and assignment or many other reasons.

I have seen people baptized with the Holy Spirit running and on fire for God, but then the fire eventually went out. They started well, but somewhere along the line, they lost touch, and although the fire went out, they have learned how to walk the walk and talk the talk, but their spiritual core is gone. The action is there, but there's no more power.

A person who was once on fire for God and went astray must learn when they come back that they shouldn't expect to immediately get back to where they once were on their own. It is only with the help of the Holy Spirit that they can get back to that level, and in yielding to Him, He can even take them higher than they were before.

The goal of this book is to help us appreciate the need for grace and learn how to tap into the grace of God when we need it. For example, if you're working with carnal people and constantly swearing, you need the grace of God to remain a Christian in their midst. You need the grace of God to remain on fire for God and still love them because some people can be very judgmental, especially regarding your Christianity.

Some believers think the only way to keep themselves pure is to build an iron wall around themselves. No! Jesus himself was around sinners and even went to the homes of tax collectors yet remained unaffected because He had access to the grace of God.

There's a song based on Zechariah 4:6 that says, *"Not by might nor by power, but by My Spirit,' says the Lord of hosts. 'This mountain shall be removed by My Spirit,' says the Lord".* You will learn how to get access to the power of the Holy Spirit to operate like a heavenly being.

If you have never been filled with the Holy Spirit, we can teach you, lay hands on you, and you will be filled and understand. But be mindful that wrong expectations will always lead to disappointment. Most people expect to start falling and breakdancing if hands are laid on them because they've seen it happen to a few people before. This is a wrong expectation because there is no scripture in the Bible to support that. Yes, it happens, but it is not the standard that the Bible has set. All the Bible says is, *When Paul laid his hands on them, they were filled with the Holy Spirit, and they began to speak in other tongues, as the Holy Spirit gave them utterance* (Acts 19:6). Therefore, the only evidence you need to know that you have received the Holy Spirit is speaking in tongues. And there is nothing mystical about speaking in tongues. It is simply speaking as the Holy Spirit gives you the utterance. You can pray in tongues while at work, and it will still be as effective and powerful as if you were speaking it in the house of God or elsewhere. But most importantly, you can enjoy fellowship with God with the Holy Spirit everywhere and as seamlessly as breathing.

Seeing, Hearing, and Knowing the Supernatural

Although grace is available, some people don't walk in it. Some people operate in more grace than others because they have connected to the channels that create access to it and stay connected.

Knowing your channel of grace is crucial, especially to thrive and navigate this season. While praying with my wife one day, I said to her that wherever you go in the world today, there is a deluge of surveillance cameras everywhere because more than ever, people want to know what is happening even when they are not around. As Christians, we have been given an innate gift from the beginning of time, which is the ability to know without the need for physical surveillance cameras. This is one of the reasons why the channels of grace are so important. The ability to know and hear what God is saying, see what is happening, and perceive in real-time so that we are not blindsided and devoid of information. How can the devil be throwing a party on your head, and you don't even know? How can the devil gather in your house and have been there for six months, and you have no idea? No dream, vision, perception, or hearing. Jesus said, "*My sheep hear My voice*" (John 10:27) and not only to hear but to know what is happening at every point in time.

We must aspire for these things, not just to discern people but also to discern and interpret events. You don't need to be in the office of a prophet to know what is happening. Everyone is first a prophet to their own lives, to know what is happening around them, especially before they happen. These are things we must aspire to know. Turn on your spiritual surveillance camera so that you'll always know what's happening. This also limits people from messing up around you because they know that you know what's happening, even though you're not there.

If you mess up around me and I haven't spoken, it's because it's not the time to speak. Judas was around Jesus for some time until the time came for Jesus to announce that a betrayer was among His disciples. The Bible says in Job 1 that when the children of God gathered, even the devil came to join them. God was clearly aware the devil attended the meeting meant for His children. How many people have you unknowingly drawn close to that you were supposed to have kept far away from your environment?

Paul said we know no man according to the flesh. How many people are you keeping in your environment based on what you see and know of them in the flesh? We must track people spiritually first to understand where they stand so that we can know how to stand with them.

So, what am I saying? We must determine if a person is good or bad. If we conclude that a person is bad, we must further investigate whether they are weak or wicked to ensure we always live a guarded life. A weak person is one with good intentions but bad outcomes. A wicked person is one with bad intentions and bad outcomes. Both weak and wicked people can wreak havoc regardless of the genuineness of their intentions. The ability to discern people is not reserved for anyone special. The Bible says God has put in the church apostles, prophets, pastors, teachers, and evangelists for the perfection of the saints so we will no longer be tossed to-and-fro by every kind of doctrine. There will be no way to worship God genuinely and not be able to experience His gifts.

There are three ways that God speaks to His people: perception (knowing), vision (seeing), and hearing (audible). Whichever one it may be for you, make sure you're always connected. Brothers and sisters, we're living in a very wicked world. For example, the world is changing daily in ways that we can never imagine, and we should be able to discern what is going on. We discern both people and events. We hear many different things from many different people. During the covid-19 pandemic, some within the body of Christ said that God was punishing mankind, while others said different and seemingly conflicting things.

But what is God saying to you? There are times when every single person may be right because they see different parts of the same elephant. Yes, God is punishing some people but is also blessing others simultaneously, just like the Israelites when they were in Egypt and were enjoying themselves. How would they interpret what was happening? They would say that God was blessing them. The Bible says that during the famine, the Israelites were being blessed. But if you asked the Egyptians the same question, they would say that God was punishing them, and they'd both be equally right.

2

Hindrances to Grace

We are advised not to pour grease down the sink because it could clog the pipe to a point where the regular liquid would no longer be able to pass through if we're not careful. Similarly, we are also advised not to flush paper towels down the toilet. For those unaware, after repeatedly doing this, the paper towel eventually builds up, and someone must reverse the blockage. Likewise, certain things can affect the flow of grace in our lives. Some things are to the flow what rubber does to electricity; they can limit and, in some cases, even completely stop that flow, whether we allow them knowingly or unknowingly. As believers, we must evaluate the things in our lives to determine what conductors like metal allow flow and insulators like rubber impede the flow.

Some of these things include carnality, outbursts of wrath, selfish ambition, distractions, and sin, and will be expounded on below.

Carnality

Carnality is the state of being fixated on the flesh and its desires. In Galatians 3:1-3, we see how Apostle Paul called out the Galatians for reverting back into fleshly things having started in the spirit. This is the same scenario that many Christians can find themselves in if adequate care is not taken.

O foolish Galatians! Who has bewitched you that you should not obey the truth, before whose eyes Jesus Christ was clearly portrayed among you as crucified? This only I want to learn from you: Did you receive the Spirit by the works of the law, or by the hearing of faith? Are you so foolish? Having begun in the Spirit, are you now being made perfect by the flesh?

What does it mean to be carnal? It means to be ruled and guided by the flesh, not by the spirit. Carnality is simply the opposite of Romans 8:14. When the spirit of God is not leading us, we are living in the flesh. Hence, a carnal person is one who is led by their flesh and its numerous destructive desires.

It's amazing because when God made man, He made him in the garden of Eden, a perfected environment. The flesh of man was not built to contend with spiritual forces. It's like taking a regular vehicle and transporting it into space, expecting it to function as it would on earth. But why would it when it was not built for that? Only the spirit can sustain spiritual things and be extremely careful that we start in the spirit and continue in the spirit. Can you imagine taking a trip and beginning in an airplane, but while flying over the middle of the ocean, the pilot announces that the remainder will be done in a sedan or on a bicycle? Sounds crazy, right? But imagine how often many people embark on a spiritual journey in the spirit, yet somewhere along the way, they yield to the flesh.

When the flesh is talking to you, it is called lust. And lust is not just reserved for sexual things, no. Your spirit can speak to you, your soul can speak to you, and your body can speak to you. We hear voices everywhere, but we must not listen to and give in to the desires of the flesh. Galatians 5:16-21 explains for as long as we are walking in the

Spirit, we shall overcome the lust of the flesh. Therefore, the key to being free from carnality is to always walk in the Spirit. When your tummy begins to rumble, your body is telling you, "I'm hungry, and you better feed me now." While it is good to eat, there is also a time to subdue the desires of the flesh by fasting. An excellent example of this is Jesus Christ. Jesus Christ fasted as led by the Holy Spirit and ate when He needed to. Many of His parables were based on food, such as when He multiplied five loaves of bread. But there were also times when he fasted.

The Bible tells us in Luke 4 that the Spirit drove Him into the wilderness, and He fasted for 40 days. If He were eating at that time, He would have been carnal. According to scripture, in the times of Ezra and Nehemiah, when they wanted to fast, God told them not to fast because they were in a time of merriment. So, in that case, if they had chosen to still fast, they would have been acting carnally. Carnality is simply doing the opposite of what the Spirit wants at every point in time. There is a time to share scripture, and there is a time to keep quiet because sharing a scripture can be a display of pride and arrogance. In 1 Corinthians 14, the Bible tells us that in the church body, when one prophet is speaking, let another keep quiet, listen, and judge. But if they all want to speak simultaneously, they are carnal and want to be braggadocious. They want to show they can hear from God and God speaks to them.

Carnality is exposed by temptation. According to James 1:14, *But each one is tempted when he is drawn away by his own desires and enticed.* How can we define what temptation is? Temptation is when the devil comes and activates, through deception, the desires of the flesh, so that we can go against what the spirit of God wants. So, we need to be extra careful but also know that the grace of God will help us resist it in Jesus's name.

The Bible says in Matthew 26:41 that *"The spirit indeed is willing, but the flesh is weak."* The flesh is not built to sustain spiritual life. If you want to fast or pray continuously in the flesh, you'll fail because it takes the enablement of the Holy Spirit. The air we breathed in yesterday was not enough to sustain us until today, so we still need to keep breathing today. I once heard someone say that "until you begin to run on God as your car runs on gas, you cannot succeed in this spiritual walk." I couldn't agree more! Why do we connect with God more actively when we are seeking something, but when we've found it, we stop connecting as aggressively as we once did?

Anyone can be a victim of carnality, especially when there is comfort. That's why you'll see that spirituality is more intense in developing nations compared to the lackluster Christianity in developed nations. There is a tendency for people to draw closer to God when they are going through challenges and have nowhere else to turn. Comfort is mainly a language of the flesh. Everything the flesh is doing is geared towards being comfortable, but the Spirit aims for closeness to God. I watched a documentary a while back that followed a group of bushmen documenting how they locate water. The men would entrap certain animals, release them, and begin to follow them. Without fail, the animals would take them to a source of water. The goal of the flesh is comfort. Not too hot, not too cold, enough food for the day. The Spirit is always aiming to locate and stay connected to God.

The Bible says in Galatians 6:6-7 to not be weary in well-doing, for in due season, you would reap if you do not lose heart. You'll reap certain things like corruption if you sow to the flesh. Similarly, you'll reap things like everlasting life if you sow to the Spirit. God will give us the grace to be able to keep sowing into the spirit in the mighty name of Jesus!

OUTBURSTS OF WRATH

While anger is not a sin, the outburst of wrath or anger is. For example, the Bible says the anger of man cannot display the righteousness of God (James 1:20). Extreme emotions like anger can pull a person out of the spiritual realm into the flesh. If you think about it, we only experience anger when our ego has been bruised. We only get hurt to the extent of an outburst when we think so highly of ourselves.

The only outburst of anger that leads to righteousness is genuinely based on the advancement of the kingdom of God. Jesus displayed this kind of anger when He chased out the money lenders and sellers from the temple. In many instances, the Pharisees, Sadducees, and Scribes attempted to get under Jesus' skin to cause Him to respond angrily, but they never succeeded. We are told to *Let love be without hypocrisy. Abhor what is evil. Cling to what is good* (Romans 12:9).

SELFISH AMBITION

Selfish ambition causes a person to believe that everything is about them. Everything they see is just about them and how they can be at the top. Some people fail to realize and accept that while they are destined for greatness, others are as well. We must be able to celebrate other people's greatness, knowing that it will not affect ours. There is no need to try to outdo other people's testimonies. The Lord spoke to me about this and said this is how pride manifests in some people. They use their testimony as an outlet for showing off, and in some cases, it can even be the reverse by some refusing to share their testimonies. But God knows the intention of everybody's heart.

Distractions

The fifth thing that can choke a person's spiritual life or the grace upon that person's life is distractions. Some people are going to and fro. Everywhere, but are nowhere. Out of the abundance of the heart, the mouth speaks. You'll have some conversations with people that will tell you the state of their mind and how they have disciplined their temperament.

Another way to define anointing or the grace of God is, concentrated power. You can never compare an hour of prayer filled with interruptions and distractions to ten minutes of uninterrupted prayer. They're not at the same level because concentration is the key. That's why you'll find that there were different times throughout Jesus' ministry where He would put everyone and everything aside to spend alone time with God. And in this era of technology, there is even more need for concentrated power. I can imagine because one of the greatest distractions in our world today is from electronic devices. The average person receives messages through multiple email accounts, text, WhatsApp, Facebook, Viber, Snapchat, Instagram, telegram, Twitter, and other apps not even listed here. A single person is tracking almost ten different channels of communication, and then there are, of course, face-to-face conversations and direct calls, which they also find important. Talk about distractions!

A few years ago, the Holy Spirit brought the benefits of living distraction-free to my attention and it led me to turn off all my notifications. You would never hear my phone ring or even vibrate, for that matter. Even a simple phone vibration can be a distraction when you are in deep meditation or in an encounter with God. There are times when we must completely disconnect from distractions to have concentrated and uninterrupted time in God's presence. We must have such uninterrupted times during each day. Even if you are the Prime Minister of Canada, the world will not come to an end if you are sometimes unreachable.

God put the passion in my heart to write *"A Disciplined Life"* because I realized that an undisciplined person could never succeed even in spiritual things. It's impossible. Here today, when they're excited, and gone tomorrow once the excitement has dissipated. And much of it is due to a lack of discipline. Distractions have to do with our mind because it is said that it is out of the abundance of the heart that the mouth speaks, and we act.

Worry is another distraction that can kill the grace of God in a person's life. In these times that we're in, people are constantly thinking about the future and what-ifs. Relax! The Bible tells us in Matthew 6:34, *"Therefore do not worry about tomorrow, for tomorrow will worry about itself. Each day has enough trouble of its own."* I used to be an extreme worrier. I had passed the bachelor's degree level in worrying many years ago and completed my master's going into a Ph.D. then God delivered me, so I had to drop my "worrying courses." I realized that what we are worried about really shows what we are in love with. We should live our lives consumed with a zeal for the house of God (John 2:17). And for the sake of clarity, the Lord's house is not just a building but also the people of God that must come first while everything else takes the backburner. You do not have to be in ministry to be consumed with zeal for the house of the Lord.

It is easy to become distracted even though you started your journey with zeal. I have always wondered why people start so well in ministry only to lose their zeal until I realized that distractions are one of the reasons why this happens. You can go on social media handles of ministers, and all you see is an emphasis on brand names and how they are enjoying the fine things in life. If you are reading this book and you have lost your zeal for Christ, return to your first love, and I pray that a fresh passion for souls will fill your heart in Jesus' name.

The Bible says God gives us good things so that we can enjoy them. But we must not enjoy them at the expense of forgetting and neglecting the Giver of the very things we are enjoying. At the time of writing this book, the COVID-19 pandemic is raging across the world. While I don't think God is behind the COVID-19 virus, I do believe that all things will work together for the good of Christ's followers. God does not tempt people with evil, so don't say that God is responsible when you are tempted because this is not the case (James 1:13). However, in every temptation, our Heavenly Father will always provide a way of escape for His children (1 Corinthians 10:13). Use every opportunity at your disposal advance the kingdom of God. Use every opportunity at your disposal to advance the vision God has given to you. Make time work for you and not against you.

Sin

The Bible tells us in Romans 6:1, *What shall we say then? Shall we continue in sin that grace may abound?* If you're living in sin and know that what you're doing is wrong, you can go through all the channels but would be wasting your time. God cannot be mocked, whatsoever a man sows, that he shall reap. Sin can take on many forms. It is not just when a person steals, lies, or commits murder that they are labelled a sinner. In fact, most people wouldn't randomly kill someone. But, if you ask them if they've ever gossiped about a person or jealously manipulated a situation to benefit themselves, they'd openly admit their actions believing it's justified and not as bad as being a murderer. Little do they know that it's the exact same thing! Sin is sin in God's eyes. There is no such thing as a big sin or a small sin.

There is no way a person can knowingly and unrepentantly live in sin and expect to reap the benefits that God has reserved for His children. That would be akin to knowingly planting weed yet expecting a bountiful harvest of corn. This is impossible. The good news is, however, 1 John 1:8-9 tells us that *if we say we have no sin, that we deceive ourselves, and the truth is not in us. If we confess our sins, He is faithful and just to forgive us our sins and to cleanse us from all unrighteousness.* But if you're living in sin, don't think you have to do something extraordinary to be forgiven. No, no, no! The beauty of our faith is the sincerity of heart and how quickly our Lord and Savior forgives. So, all that is required is for you to say, "Lord, I'm sorry. I'm sorry. I know I messed up, and I'm sorry." That's it. It is that simple, and with this forgiveness, you now have access to the channels of grace.

When you connect with the God of all the earth, you can never be the same. The problem is many people only know God based on what people say. They don't have faith in God because they don't know God. How can you have faith in someone you're not connected to? God forbid, if a pastor makes a mistake, then your faith will fail. That's why when some pastors fall or backslide, they take a multitude of people with them. However, a person who knows God for themselves would know not to put the entirety of their trust in man and that the only perfect person to have walked this earth is Jesus Christ.

3

Channels of Grace

When I first came to Christ, I had so much of the law mentality, trying to do things on my own, and kept falling flat. Weeks would go by, and it would seem like I was moving forward, then things came crashing down until I received the revelation of Zechariah 4:6 that says, *'Not by might nor by power, but by My spirit,'* says the Lord of hosts. From that moment on, I stopped trying to accomplish things with my own strength.

To please God takes the grace of God. The Bible says in Hebrew 4:15 that Jesus was tempted in the same way we all are tempted, and in James 5:17 that Elijah was a man with a nature like ours. It was really the grace of God that came in and made them extraordinary. How could they have accomplished some such extraordinary things on their own? No one can consistently do anything spiritually without the grace of God because it's His grace that enables us to function effectively.

Grace is simply help from above, and in this New Testament era, God has made it available because He wants us to do everything He has commanded us to do. If a person is willing enough to take the first step, God will give them the grace to do everything they need to do. The grace to pray, fast, forgive, serve, live holy, and even give.

If you want to serve God diligently in this age of distractions, you need the grace of God. Many people make new year commitments but don't follow through, how much more their commitments to the things of God. Paul mentions in 1 Corinthians 15:10, *But by the grace of God I am what I am, and His grace toward me was not in vain; but I labored more abundantly than they all, yet not I, but the grace of God which was with me.* The grace of God allows a person to function at a higher dimension, where the things that were once difficult to do become easy to do. You can relate this to a truck carrying a heavy load compared to a sedan carrying the same load. Although the load is the same, their results are different because the truck's engine has more capacity than the sedan and, therefore, can push the load seamlessly. This is grace!

Another example of grace at work is from a testimony shared by a church member who was in school at the time. The individual mentioned that he didn't have enough time to study, so he asked God specifically for strength. He went for days without sleeping, needing coffee or energy drinks and redeemed his time to study. Don't think the grace of God is something theoretical; it is very much tangible and practical.

In 2 Corinthians 12:7-9, Paul was feeling weak because of a thorn in his flesh, a messenger of Satan to withstand, but the grace of God made him stand strong. The scripture reads, *and lest I should be exalted above measure by the abundance of the revelations, a thorn in the flesh was given to me, a messenger of Satan to buffet me, lest I be exalted above measure. Concerning this thing I pleaded with the Lord three times that it might depart from me. And He said to me, "My grace is sufficient for you, for My strength is made perfect in weakness." Therefore, most gladly I will rather boast in my infirmities, that the power of Christ may rest upon me.* Sometimes the difficulty may not be taken away, but instead, God will give us the grace to deal with it as He did with Paul in this situation. Moses experienced something similar. God never removed his stammering, but instead, He gave Him the grace to do what He called Him to do. What is it that you're struggling with? Keep it in mind as you read this book, take it to God, and ask Him for grace.

Some of us are using other people's weapons and it's not working for us. You do your devotion for one week and you stop because you're not getting results. You're struggling to access God through other people's channels of grace and leave feeling dejected, discouraged, and disappointed then begin to feel like an outcast and rejected by God. And now you're left wondering why, giving the step room to step in and say, "It's because of what you did before you were born. Ask for forgiveness, and then you'll be fine." Then you ask for forgiveness, but the next day there's another reason, and another reason and the cycle continue.

You may be asking, "but can I use a different channel of grace aside from my natural one?" and the answer is yes, there is an exception. When it comes to the channels of grace, the one exception to using another would be based on the instructions of the Holy Spirit. We are naturally designed to breathe through our nostrils, but we can breathe through our mouths when things are not functioning properly. Similarly, your main channel is what you would use primarily to quickly ascend into God's presence, but there can be exceptions. Be mindful that there's a reason why God gave every one of us our own channel of grace. Part of the issue within the body of Christ is the frustration that comes when we try to force ourselves through an unnatural channel.

And as we begin to dive deeper, always remember that we are not celebrating the channels; we are celebrating our access to the throne of grace.

Accessing Grace

When a car is low on fuel, it's obvious to many people to fuel up at the gas station to continue driving. Similarly, whenever you find yourself under pressure, anxious, or worrisome, that's an indication that you need grace. If you're struggling in any area as a Christian, even though you desire to please God, your missing link is grace. You cannot expect not to struggle with your devotions if you're following a system without the spirit. All God wants from you is your willingness, and the grace will come afterwards. Hebrews 4:16 instructs us, saying, *let us therefore come boldly to the throne of grace, that we may obtain mercy and find grace to help in time of need.* Likewise, Matthew 11:28-30 also instructs us; *"Come to Me, all you who labor and are heavy laden, and I will give you rest. Take My yoke upon you and learn from Me, for I am gentle and lowly in heart, and you will find rest for your souls. For My yoke is easy and My burden is light."* One of the ways you'll know that you have spent time with God is by how light you'll feel afterwards. We don't have to carry our burdens alone; we can exchange them and take up His light yoke instead.

You must understand that grace is not assumed to be given; it must be consciously sought after. God has made grace available and wants to help you, but don't wait for Him to come to you. You must go to Him and obtain it. Only a demonic spirit will possess a person without their permission, according to Mark 5:1-2, but the Holy Ghost requires your permission. The Bible says in James 4:6 that "God resists the proud but gives grace to the humble." While it is an act of humility to ask God for help, you'd be shocked by how many people find this difficult to do because they want to impress God. We can't impress God. We are made by grace, sustained by grace, and we excel by grace, so we cannot take the glory for anything God does through us.

When we were about to give the $300,000 plus deposit on our first church, I knew what was in the church's account and how and when resources started getting supplied. As we began the renovation process, it got to a point where God instructed me to protect my faith by not looking at the church's bank account again but to keep moving. His words were, "stop monitoring the account to see what's inside; so that when I tell you something, you don't understand it based on what you see in the account." As we kept moving, things just kept being provided. When you know how you've gotten to a particular place that seemed impossible initially, it becomes insanity or unimaginable to take the glory for what God has done. It is by grace, not by strength. Don't get me wrong, some people succeed by their own strength, but at great costs. Either at the expense of their relationships, family, or their health. But there are no adverse side effects when the grace of God is at work in a person's life.

If you understand how planes work, you'll know that a plane's cabin is pressurized to provide a safe and comfortable environment for passengers and crew when flying at high altitudes. The higher the plane flies, the more atmospheric pressure the plane experiences. Pressurization makes it possible for human beings to survive at high altitude. This analogy is like what grace can do for you. The higher you go in life, the more the pressure you will face. Pressure, however, does not have to lead to stress. You can be operating in a high-pressure environment and still be able to laugh, joke and function normally because of the grace of God at work in your life. Receive the grace of God, now in Jesus' name!

What are the Channels of Grace?

The Bible mentions severally that God answers prayers, but not too many people can provide evidence of answered prayers in their lives. It is said in Numbers 23:19 that *"God is not a man, that He should lie."* So why is it that the promises of God aren't evidenced in many people's lives? The problem is that many people know the "what" but don't know the "how." They know that God provides yet they still suffer lack.

They know that God gives grace, yet many of them are still drowning in stress. The revelation I am about to share with you has transformed my relationship with God, and I pray that it would do the same for you in Jesus' name.

In Matthew 11:28-30 and Hebrews 4:16, we are encouraged to seek God's grace as we go through life. If you are wondering how to approach God for that grace, ensure you are highly focused and receptive as you read this section.

Grace is available in abundance, and God, in His infinite wisdom, has established different means by which we can obtain that grace. This revelation came to me a few years ago and is what we now know as the channels of grace. There are many ways to understand this revelation, and I'll give a few examples throughout this book. Hold onto the one you're able to connect with as you continue reading.

The channels of grace are access points to the power of God and are a unique approach that God has given us to have access to Him. You can picture it as a road we have to travel on to get to the treasure house of grace. One thing you must settle in your heart is that God is not a wicked God. Years ago, someone told me that their brother said to them that in the western world if you're trying to do something and it is difficult to get it done, you're most likely doing it the wrong way. Think of the silliest and even the most straightforward way, and most likely, that is the way it is supposed to be done. Some people believe that they must labor extensively for everything in life, so if anything seems too simple, they've rationalized in their mind that it is incorrect. In like manner, from the moment we give our lives to Jesus, God has already given us a back door that will make it extremely easy for us to find Him, except if the devil steps in to mess things up.

Imagine there were five doors that could give you access to a specific room, and you had the key to one of those doors. Unless you were told which door that key could open, you'd go through a process of trial and error before you find the door that easily opens when you insert the key. With the newfound knowledge that the key you have works for that particular door, you would most likely go through that same door because of how easy it was to enter. Now let's say your door got jammed, and you want to enter that room but have no choice but to enter through another door. You can go with one of two options: you can allow someone else who has the key to that door to let you in or decide to pick the lock on the door. It's clear that the first option will give you faster access than trying to pick the lock yourself. God has designed each one of us to have keys to open different doors. The keys, in this case, represent the various channels of grace, the door represents the entry point, and the room is God's throne room of grace.

God has built natural things into every one of us that will make it easy for us to access grace if we utilize them correctly and consistently. For some people, prayer is like washing dishes. They don't want to wash dishes, but because they need to eat on a clean plate, they will only wash one plate and use that one. Whereas some love it so much that the moment a dish is put in the sink, they just wash it immediately. For some of us, God must pull the worship out of our mouths, while for some people, it just comes very easy for them. This is the joy in my heart about the channels of grace; everybody can connect in their own unique way. God is no respecter of persons; if you don't connect with your channel of grace, you will find it difficult to connect easily with Him daily. It's important for us to understand these things; otherwise, we'll push back on what God has easily given us and consequently force ourselves towards something unnatural, thus making us feel as if we aren't attaining much.

When you go through scripture and see people who connected with God on a deep level, you'll notice that they had certain channels they used the most to connect with God. For example, Elisha's was worship, Elijah's was meditation, and Jeremiah's was the word of God.

Some people, all they know is they like nature and feel at peace when they are around nature. All they are saying is their channel of grace is meditation which we will explore later.

If you are trying to go to a city, there are questions you'll ask yourself, whether intentionally or unintentionally. Where am I going? How do I get to where I am going? What is the fastest way to get there? You may arrive by plane, car, bus, or train, but which mode of transportation will get you to your destination the fastest? This is the concept behind the channels of grace. If you forget anything along the way, just remember that God has already programmed in you what will make it easy for you to find Him.

Note: Once you have found your channel of grace, do not compare your channel with someone else's channel. Do not neglect the channel you have been naturally given by God. Locate your channel of grace and cultivate it so that you can walk with God with ease. Remember that I am not encouraging you to forsake other channels of grace. The revelation this book is bringing into the body of Christ is the uniqueness of each person in their quest to connect with the Father of all spirits (Hebrews 12:9) and how that uniqueness should be prioritized and emphasized when we seek God.

Without further ado, let's deep dive into the different channels of grace so you can obtain the grace you need.

The Channel of Association

Many of us have treasures that we never utilize, and one of such treasures is the gift of people. For many of us, the answers we go around the world seeking can easily be answered by people already in our lives. This channel of grace is simply the innate ability to draw grace from others as we fellowship with them. I have observed that many evangelists operate in the association channel of grace.

In Proverbs 27:17, the Bible refers to the phenomenon of iron sharpening iron - *As iron sharpens iron, so one person sharpens another.* This is the same way some phones can now be charged by placing it on another phone. That is essentially what the channel of association is. A person functioning in this channel will have the natural ability to connect deeply with others and for others to connect deeply with them. Do not immediately think that this is not your channel because you're an introvert. An introvert is simply a person who draws energy from small gatherings while an extrovert draws energy from larger gatherings.

The first instance where a person was filled with the Holy Ghost outside the disciples happened in Luke 1:39-45. John the Baptist was filled with the Holy Spirit while still in his mother, Elizabeth's womb. The moment the pregnant Elizabeth heard Mary's voice, the son in her womb received a baptism of the Holy Spirit.

Now Mary arose in those days and went into the hill country with haste, to a city of Judah, and entered the house of Zacharias and greeted Elizabeth. And it happened, when Elizabeth heard the greeting of Mary, that the babe leaped in her womb; and Elizabeth was filled with the Holy Spirit. Then she spoke out with a loud voice and said, "Blessed are you among women, and blessed is the fruit of your womb! But why is this granted to me, that the mother of my Lord should come to me? For indeed, as soon as the voice of your greeting sounded in my ears, the babe leaped in my womb for joy. Blessed is she who believed, for there will be a fulfillment of those things which were told to her from the Lord."

Do you know how many conversations we have heard or have had, and no grace has been released? To benefit from this channel, you must succeed in walking in love, as offence cuts the connection to grace. Understand that a person can laugh with you on the outside, but harbour offence on the inside, which will cause grace not to flow. I'm talking about genuine love, which has nothing to do with proximity.

There are voices you hear that can strengthen you and empower you. Sometimes they might say things that you already know, but it's not the words where the grace lies; it's the spirit behind the words. When we speak, we are communicating with spirits. John 6:63 says, *"The words that I speak to you are spirit, and they are life."* In the case of association, just being around or connected to that person gives you strength and energy. It's one of the reasons why people like to be around loved ones. In fact, they will tell a person who has a terminal illness to have their family around them. Why? Because it strengthens them and gives them the will to live. It's one of the reasons why the Bible says we should not be unequally yoked.

Association can draw energy from you, so we need to be aware of that. There are people like that in the animal kingdom, and we call them parasites. All they do is draw from you. You're charged, but you become drained the moment you talk to that person. I love that passage of scripture in John 4, Jesus was ministering to the Samaritan woman. He wasn't connecting with her. Those are two different things. You can minister to anybody so long as you're not receiving from them. You'll see that when Jesus was communicating with the Samaritan woman, He wasn't responding to what she was saying. He would say one thing, she would bring up an argument, and He would jump to something else. She was looking for a fight because she was living in offence. According to Bible scholars, she was out there to draw water in the heat of the day because she didn't have friends. Generally, they used to go to the well together in that culture. She couldn't go with people because they refused to befriend her as she was known for taking people's husbands. She was going alone and found Jesus with that offensive spirit.

I can minister to anybody, but when it comes to associating with people, that's a different story entirely. Once I start associating with someone, the moment I see I was drained and it happens a second time, there will never be a third time. I don't know anyone who would allow a thief to remain in their vicinity, and that's exactly what happens if you are left drained after associating with a person.

We must avoid offence with association because it can affect the connection. Jesus and the woman who touched the hem of His garment had a connection. You can classify it as an attraction, and that attraction draws virtue from one party to the other. May God give us the wisdom to choose our association wisely, in Jesus' name! Amen!

Why is it that a person can be in the same church or house as someone else and have feelings of hatred or dislike towards the other person? In Exodus 26 and 27, there was a way God told Moses to build the tabernacle. It had the inner court, the outer court, and the holies of holies, which was the holiest place. The grace that comes through association depends on the category of people with whom you're associating. What we receive from each person in these different categories is not the same, which is why offence from someone in your holies of holies, such as a spouse or a loved one, can cut deeper than an average person. God should be at the center of your holies of holies, but we cannot keep deceiving ourselves that we will only get grace from Him. The truth is, sometimes the grace won't come vertically (above) but will come horizontally (beside). The Ethiopian Eunuch in Acts 8 was on the road reading the book of Isaiah, but God never clarified the word to him; he sent Philip instead. Now, I'm not saying to skip connecting with God; but ensure you don't forsake the gathering of saints as instructed in Hebrews 10:25.

The church is a treasure-house of grace, comprising of the five-fold ministries (the apostle, the prophet, the evangelist, the pastor, and the teacher), and every believer is called into at least one of the offices. There is something soothing about interacting with someone with a Pastoral gift. You feel loved and safe, even when you initially felt condemned prior to speaking with them. That is grace being transferred. One of the ways you know something is by grace is that anybody can partake of it. There is a grace donor and a grace recipient. A person who has the associative grace has the natural ability to pull grace from others, even without their permission, if they want to. Again, this is another reason why the bible says that we should not be unequally yoked.

The Channel of Faith in the Word

"Most assuredly, I say to you, the hour is coming, and now is, when the dead will hear the voice of the Son of God; and those who hear will live. For as the Father has life in Himself, so He has granted the Son to have life in Himself" (John 5:25-26)

God has put in some people a natural grace and love for the Word of God. These people are natural bookworms and avid readers. Some may not realize it because their reading is currently things like blogs and gossip sites instead of books, but it is a misused gift. It's a natural grace for information. A gossiper is simply someone whose channel of grace is most likely the word. But the enemy has been able to assault that gifting or channel of grace and has caused them to move in a different direction by utilizing it negatively.

While gossip is sweet to some, others are way more connected to gossip than others. For instance, they can forget that they were cooking because of how carried away they got by the gossip. These people will seek and trade gossip daily. If you want to know anything about another person, they'll quickly supply you with that information. Perhaps that is someone God has naturally graced to connect with Him through the Word. If you are currently under the influence of gossip, I declare you delivered in Jesus' name.

Some people are quick to believe everything people say. You may label them as gullible, but in many cases, those are people God has naturally gifted the ability to believe. Of course, they must grow in wisdom to discern between good and evil, but they are prime candidates for drawing energy through the Word. We hear words every day, but without faith in the Word of God, the power would not be disseminated or discharged the way it ought to be.

Let's remind ourselves what grace is. We can say grace is strength, energy, unmerited favour, and power to go beyond our natural capacity. When we need something to move forward, but we're burnt out and tired at different levels, we know that grace is what we need. Sleep is not always the solution when seeking for physical strength as there are times when you can sleep and wake up the next day still feeling tired. Vacations aren't always the answer either because some people return from vacations even more tired and feel like they need another vacation. You can sometimes excitedly go to work only to encounter a coworker and immediately feel like quitting your job. And yes, there are times when this may be the case when God is leading you elsewhere. But often, you don't need another job; all you need is grace to stay in your place of assignment.

When you study the book of Ezekiel thoroughly, you'll see that his primary channel of grace was the Word:

The word of the Lord came expressly to Ezekiel the priest, the son of Buzi, in the land of the Chaldeans by the River Chebar; and the hand of the Lord was upon him there. (Ezekiel 1:3)

Then the Spirit entered me when He spoke to me, and set me on my feet; and I heard Him who spoke to me. (Ezekiel 2:2)

In Ezekiel 1:3, we see that the word of the Lord first came upon Ezekiel before the hand of the Lord came upon Him. It was the same hand upon Ezekiel that came upon Elijah and caused him to run faster than the chariots of Ahab. So, Elijah received grace for speed when the hand of God came upon him. Samson received grace for physical strength when the spirit of God came upon him. In the second passage, Ezekiel got strengthened when he received the word that came forth. The key to operating in this channel of grace is faith. Faith has a response to the Word. It's not deliberating or analyzing the Word; it is believing the Word. Grace is released when we act on the word spoken by God. The Word of God always has power, but we tap into that power when we submit our will to what the Word of God says. It's an instruction. This is called the response of faith.

During the renovation process of our first church building, the Lord told me, "Sit back and allow Me to finish the church building." So, what did I do? I believed because I received an instruction, not a suggestion. After that, whenever I saw a mountain, I remembered the Word "sit back." Eventually, a way came, turning that mountain into a molehill. God always makes a way.

Someone said that any faith that is not practical is fake, which is entirely accurate. We need to see in action where the Word becomes flesh, as mentioned in John 1:14. This is why I love the practicality of our faith. People can fall ill while we are perfectly healthy, walking in divine health. That's faith in action. Faith in action is walking in divine health while others are falling ill. In this economy, people are going broke, but God is making way for us to be expanded and promoted while others complain about being overlooked. When you look at first responders, they run toward a dangerous situation while others run away from it. We are to be like first responders as believers. If you really received the word, it must determine the actions you take or don't take.

Look at what happened when Peter received the words from Jesus in Matthew 14:25-33,

> *Now in the fourth watch of the night Jesus went to them, walking on the sea. And when the disciples saw Him walking on the sea, they were troubled, saying, "It is a ghost!" And they cried out of fear. But immediately, Jesus spoke to them, saying, "Be of good cheer! It is I; do not be afraid." And Peter answered Him and said, "Lord, if it is You, command me to come to You on the water." So He said, "Come." And when Peter had come down out of the boat, he walked on the water to go to Jesus. But when he saw that the wind was boisterous, he was afraid; and beginning to sink, he cried out, saying, "Lord, save me!" And immediately, Jesus stretched out His hand and caught him, and said to him, "O you of little faith, why did you doubt?" And when they got into the boat, the wind ceased. Then those who were in the boat came and worshiped Him, saying, "Truly You are the Son of God."*

You can laugh at Peter, but the fact remains that he walked on water, albeit for a short period. But the key here is that grace was released when he believed what Jesus said without asking for the mathematical equation of how possible it is to walk on water. Jesus said come, and because he believed, he went. When you put your faith in the Word of God, it will supply the energy you need to keep moving forward. You cannot receive inspiration from God and suffer from expiration. Constant inspiration from the Word will eliminate expiration from life.

Jesus had three key disciples He took to certain places: Peter, James, and John. They were all aware of their God-given channel of grace. Peter's channel of grace was faith in the Word. When you study Peter, both during the ministry of Christ and afterward, you'll see that most of the grace he operated in was through faith in the word, while John's channel of grace was association.

You see, it is one thing to know what God can make available to us, but people who don't know how to get there will always be at the devil's mercy because they're dwelling in ignorance. He'll tell them, "You're fasting, you're praying, but God is not talking to you. Look at how He's talking to that other person, or this person, or that person". "How come God hasn't done this? How come God hasn't done that?" If they're not careful, they can begin to face discouragement, which would have caused their faith to dwindle. Can you imagine if Judas was one of those in the top three? He would have killed Jesus from the inside. Jesus could not be around unstable people; it would've been dangerous and detrimental to His ministry and assignment.

When Jesus asked His disciples who they thought He was, Peter answered, "you're the Christ, Son of the Living God." Then Jesus replied, "flesh and blood did not reveal this to you." Those with revelation of who God is are the ones who can be in His inner caucus. Because of their revelation of who God is, they can connect with Him. Peter connected with Christ through his revelation of Christ's true identity, and this word solidified Peter's faith. The revelation of Jesus' identity is what kept Peter stable as a faithful disciple. Genuine and long-lasting strength only comes from connecting with God. It is only when you have a genuine connection with God that you can in turn maintain genuine relationships. The genuineness of Peter's relationship with Jesus is what made Jesus pray for Peter and not Judas when they were both tempted by the devil.

For those that claim to have a prophetic ministry and don't study the Word, what they have and are prophesying is a joke. The real key to discerning spirits is the Word of God. Once you continually meditate on the Word, you'll find that you're able to discern between good and evil. You'll just know. Whether you pay attention to it or not is up to you.

For the word of God is living and powerful, and sharper than any two-edged sword, piercing even to the division of soul and spirit, and of joints and marrow, and is a discerner of the thoughts and intents of the heart (Hebrews 4:12).

When I started hearing from God, I was meditating on the Word, and then I just heard a voice tell me, "Send a message to that leader and tell him this and this." I sent the message, and the response was shocking. The person was shocked, saying, "wow, how did you know? I was on my break pondering on that same thought!". Grace is released once the word is spoken and must be acted on immediately. There is a time factor when it comes to receiving grace from the Word of God. When God says, "jump," there's a time factor attached. When He says move, He means to move right then, not two years later. If you move two years later, you're moving in your strength, not the strength of the Holy Spirit.

When I say faith in the Word is a channel of grace, I don't mean the entire Bible because even the devil knows the Bible. It is the word that God reveals to you from the Bible that gives you life. This life is what I refer to as grace.

For the word of God is living and powerful, and sharper than any two-edged sword, piercing even to the division of soul and spirit, and of joints and marrow, and is a discerner of the thoughts and intents of the heart (Hebrews 4:12).

When I started hearing from God, I was meditating on the Word, and then I just heard a voice tell me, "Send a message to that leader and tell him this and this." I sent the message, and the response was shocking. The person was shocked, saying, "wow, how did you know? I was on my break pondering on that same thought!". Grace is released once the word is spoken and must be acted on immediately. There is a time factor when it comes to receiving grace from the Word of God. When God says, "jump," there's a time factor attached. When He says move, He means to move right then, not two years later. If you move two years later, you're moving in your strength, not the strength of the Holy Spirit.

When I say faith in the Word is a channel of grace, I don't mean the entire Bible because even the devil knows the Bible. It is the word that God reveals to you from the Bible that gives you life. This life is what I refer to as grace.

"It is the Spirit who gives life; the flesh profits nothing. The words that I speak to you are spirit, and they are life" (John 6:63).

So many institutions study the Bible but don't study to connect with faith in the Word. The Bible is a package, but it's not the only package of the Word of God. Memorizing scripture is not the same thing as faith in the Word. I know of someone who was fearfully running away from a dog, yet quoting 2 Timothy 1:7, so memorizing is not the same as faith. When you have faith and the word moves into your spirit, it does something to you. You'll then understand that it is no longer by power nor by might but the Word and the Spirit driving your actions. Many years ago, the Lord told me that "change is constant, and in every change, there will be winners and losers. But you will always be a winner." So anytime I see a change, I remember that word, and receive strength.

Many of us think the word of God is very cheap. I'm not talking about information. I'm talking about impartation and revelation. The Bible says in Matthew 13:11, *"Because it has been given to you to know the mysteries of the kingdom of heaven."* Jesus said to the disciples, "some people wanted to see what you see and hear what you hear, but it was not given to them." Daniel fasted for days waiting for the word of the Lord. The Prince of Persia captured the Word, and the King of Persia resisted the messenger until an archangel helped him, and he succeeded. This resistance was because the angel was carrying a word for Daniel, which shows the value of the Word of God. The devil knows those that have the Word in certain areas. Unless you lose it, he won't even mess with you in those areas.

There's a lady God gave a word to that, "they will never have an accident." She has had many near misses, but even the devil knows that person cannot have an accident because God had already spoken the word years ago. Once you understand this, you will never approach God casually to get the word from Him.

Each of the channels we will explore in this book have requirements that need to be met to draw grace. In the channel of association, we said a person must avoid offence and walk in love. For the channel of faith in the Word, a person must go through a process of preparation before receiving the grace packaged in the Word. We see this in the story of Elijah in 1 Kings 19:11-18,

Then He said, "Go out, and stand on the mountain before the Lord." And behold, the Lord passed by, and a great and strong wind tore into the mountains and broke the rocks in pieces before the Lord, but the Lord was not in the wind; and after the wind an earthquake, but the Lord was not in the earthquake; and after the earthquake a fire, but the Lord was not in the fire; and after the fire a still small voice. So it was, when Elijah heard it, that he wrapped his face in his mantle and went out and stood in the entrance of the cave. Suddenly a voice came to him, and said, "What are you doing here, Elijah? And he said, "I have been very zealous for the Lord God of hosts; because the children of Israel have forsaken Your covenant, torn down Your altars, and killed Your prophets with the sword. I alone am left, and they seek to take my life."Then the Lord said to him: "Go, return on your way to the

Wilderness of Damascus; and when you arrive, anoint Hazael as king over Syria. Also you shall anoint Jehu, the son of Nimshi, as king over Israel. And Elisha, the son of Shaphat of Abel Meholah, you shall be anointed as prophet in your place. It shall be that whoever escapes the sword of Hazael, Jehu will kill; and whoever escapes the sword of Jehu, Elisha will kill. Yet I have reserved seven thousand in Israel, all whose knees have not bowed to Baal, and every mouth that has not kissed him."

Do you see the number of things Elijah had to go through just to receive a still, small voice? It's like going to a fancy restaurant where it takes a long time before the food comes. Or, like a coconut that you must keep hitting to get the flesh and water trapped on the inside. You'll realize the worth of going through the process only after you've tasted it. The word will come in crumbs if this is your primary channel of grace. Some of us get that little shock of energy like what you get from energy bars, and while this isn't real food, it gives you enough energy until you can get real food. Elijah heard many voices, but it was leading up to the main prize, which was the instruction about his successor. In like manner, you can get a word during a message, but that is just there to push you to get enough strength to go on a retreat to seek God.

Before Elijah received the Word of the Lord, he was troubled and running away because of Jezebel, but during his interaction with God, he did not say anything about her. I can assure you that the moment Elijah got the instructions from God, he forgot about Jezebel, and she was no longer an issue. The moment you have that word and have allowed it to enter your spirit, you become like God in that area. Therefore, it's not something that comes casually. For example, those that have gotten that word from God that no devil can kill them if they believe it, there can be a fatal plane crash, but that person will survive. It's funny how people believe in magic more than they believe in scripture.

The difference between this channel of grace and others is preparation. You must prepare yourself to search for the word you need. When David went to Ziklag and saw that the Amalekites had taken his family and destroyed their things, the Bible said that David strengthened himself in the Lord before he went to get the word of the Lord. Although you may need gas, you need to have at least enough to get you to the gas station. With other channels of grace, you can remain there and fill up, but with the channel of grace through the Word, you need extra gas in your tank to take you there. Do you remember the story of the five wise virgins and the five foolish virgins? The five wise virgins had extra oil, which is part of the wisdom for profitable living. Have extra, and do not wait until your tank is empty. That's why in 1 Kings 19, when Elijah was burnt out and was running away from Jezebel, he had to sleep to get strength. The angel woke him up twice to eat for strength and to get the Word. This is why I tell people to rest before they come to our Friday night prayers. Imagine if Elijah didn't get enough sleep. Do you think he would've been able to capture all the instructions God gave him? No. The angel could have given him the word directly, but that was not what was needed then. He needed to be sharp and well-rested so that when God spoke to him, he could pick exactly what God was saying. He didn't have to return and ask God to please repeat Himself.

I heard a story that Bishop Oyedepo's son was sharing of himself. He works with his father in the ministry and said that every time his father sends for him, he goes with a notepad and a pen so that he won't have to go back and say, "sorry, I missed something you said." And I thought, what level of discipline he has! No wonder why some people are where they are. Some people don't write anything down because they believe their minds are supercomputers, but they assume one thing and miss other things, then blame God. When you have visitations and wake up in the middle of the night, write them down. Something has convinced you, "don't worry, go back to sleep. When you wake up, you'll remember it very well". If it has happened not once, not twice, and you've forgotten, what makes you think you'll remember this time or the next? Let's apply wisdom to document these things.

Let me give you some advice, never come to the presence of God casually. You will always get something, but why come to get a little when what is available is so much more? As for me, I value time so much that I can't imagine coming to do something "just because" when I have other things I could be doing. So, when you're in the presence of God, make the best use of it. Start by preparing your mind. You can pray, "Lord, I'm going to hear a word today. Lord, I need You to answer my question today. You know what I need." And when you don't know what you need, just ask Him, "tell me something I need to know for this season of my life. Lord, I don't want to appear casually. I must hear something that will transform my life and move me from one level to another."

I heard a man of God say that when he speaks to his spiritual mom – his spiritual dad has passed away – he's on his knees as she speaks over the phone to position himself properly to hear and understand what is being said. My wife and I spent time with our spiritual parents last year. And while we were in the office, he was talking when he said the word 'system' God just began to bring a flood of revelation on systems. This is where the message of interconnected systems came along with many other things. Just from that one word he mentioned in a sentence, God began to speak, and from that encounter has now become a book.

We shouldn't approach the Word of God casually, whether directly, through an anointed vessel or an anointed book. The Lord said to me many years ago, "never read the Bible casually; otherwise, you'll just have a casual experience." So, before I read, I say, "Father, open my eyes to see wonderful things. Speak to me, oh Lord, from what I've never seen before, in Jesus' name". You'll see that you can read the same passage, and suddenly, you'll see that things are jumping out from everywhere you never noticed previously. Once you believe what the Word of God has said, the power is released, and nobody can stop you nor will stop you in the name of Jesus Christ!

The Channel of Prayer

Let us therefore come boldly to the throne of grace, that we may obtain mercy and find grace to help in time of need. (Hebrews 4:16)

What is prayer? Prayer is communicating with God, and the content of that communication varies. It can be a prayer of inquiry or a prayer of supplication where we ask for material things or protection. But regardless of the type of prayer, it is simply communication with God.

Sometimes we avoid prayer because we have this grandiose idea of what prayer is. We often think about the ritual of prayer instead of the content itself. You don't always have to kneel somewhere for you to pray. When people ask me about getting married and how to do it, I say the essence of marriage is just handing over custody of a woman to a man, which can be done in 2 minutes. Seriously! But many people neglect this part because they are interested in the ritual of marriage (walking down the aisle, the outfits, the reception, etc.), and this is the same mindset people have regarding prayer. The main content of prayer is what God is looking at and the state of our hearts.

You may ask, shouldn't there be a ritual around approaching God or a way to package yourself when going to God? In many homes, especially traditional African homes, the mother is the way to the father. You dare not go to the father directly to ask him anything. The mother will tell you the right time and way, but in my opinion, that is not ideal because that is deception. The better and wise route to take is through the Holy Spirit. The Holy Spirit knows the mind of God. He knows when to bring in certain requests to the Father. There are times when I would be praying and would sense the Holy Spirit nudging me to ask

God for whatever I want in my spirit. There is a way to package yourself when going to God; we need to understand that there are different types of prayers. In an educational institution, you'll see that you used to have casual interactions, but when it's time to attend graduation, you'll notice that things are more formal and structured. Likewise, we must understand that there is a time for everything when it comes to prayer. There are prayers that are casual, and there are prayers where you must go through some set of procedures. But all those prayers are acceptable to God so long as we follow the correct procedure.

Imagine a newborn that has yet to learn the culture or that there is a bathroom to pass out waste. The parents will come – I hope gladly – to clean them up. But as the child grows, passing out waste wherever and whenever becomes unacceptable because they have learned the protocol of going to the bathroom themselves. This is similar to a believer's prayer life. Certain prayers may be acceptable, while others may not be acceptable based on your level of growth with God.

Some people can pray casually, and God will hear, and for some, if they pray that same prayer, God will not hear because He expects more from them. For example, when you look at the children of Israel, they disrespected God numerous times, and God forgave them, but God told Moses to speak to the rock, and he hit the rock, and God got angry. You might be wondering, does God have double standards? No, it's the level of growth and exposure He had given to Moses. He will, therefore, require more from you based on how much of Himself that He has revealed to you. But this all boils down to conviction.

I remember years ago in a different ministry; there was a time when a gospel minister with a prophetic gift that I had known previously was coming. I talked to God in prayer, setting my expectations for that meeting. I asked God, saying, "I want this man to call me up and prophesy to me." This was around the time when the instruction concerning Cornerstone was coming from God, so I needed that validation. I said,

"God, I want him to tell me to stand up out of everybody, and I'll believe that You are the one calling me." I kept praying that prayer, and one day God said to me, "shut up, not everybody can pray those types of prayers, and I accept it. You hear from Me, so I don't need to tell him to prophesy in front of everybody for you to believe, but some people need that." I said, "Okay, I'm sorry," and the meeting continued. On the last day, the minister did a demonstration and called some people out, including me. At a particular point in that demonstration, several of us were across the stage area. The minister then casually said, "For example, God is saying 'go and build Me a church for the next generation,'". Immediately the minister uttered those words, Holy Spirit said, "okay, that is you I'm talking to now."

Our relationship with God determines the protocol for prayer and how much of Himself He has exposed to us. In this dispensation, we must be close to the Holy Spirit. He is our counsellor and must be the ultimate counsellor, while everyone else augments what He is doing in our lives. Sometimes the teachings are just there to help make sense of what the Holy Spirit says. I'm not saying that you can't have a casual conversation with God when you get to a particular point with God. I'm saying that at a point where, based on the leading of the Holy Spirit, you'll know the kind of prayer protocol required in every situation. For example, the Bible says we should not be hasty to lay hands. Someone at a particular level of growth in God may just know one way of healing, but you see in the ministry of Jesus when He was healing people, He did it in different ways, not just by the laying of hands. They say to a carpenter that everything is a hammer and nails, but the more you grow, the more you realize that there are different tools at your disposal.

If you've been driving a car for quite some time, you know how the car works. If you get into the car one day and try to start it, but the vehicle is not starting, you will know that something is wrong. John 10:27 says, "My sheep hear My voice." Here simply means my sheep can communicate with Me. The moment you see that for some time you're doing what you're used to doing and not getting results, then you must stop and ask questions. "Holy Spirit, what is going on? This is not the way it's supposed to be". I'll give you an example. When Jesus was on the cross, He was used to communing with God, and it got to a point where He said, "Father, why have you forsaken Me?" The nature of that question does not require an answer, but He said that because He knew something was not the way it was supposed to be. Many of us realize something is wrong, but we keep going in the same direction. I heard the definition of insanity is doing the same thing repeatedly and expecting a different result. In my understanding, that's where religion is born; when you're not getting results, but you keep doing the same thing because that's what you've been taught. For example, if you've been praying and praying and asking questions, but you've never gotten an answer, why are you still doing the same things and making excuses upon excuses, yet hearing people share testimonies of them hearing from God? You need to stop and ask questions. "God, is it only that you talk to some people? Is it that I've not reached a point where You can speak to me? Is it that you're speaking to me, but I don't understand?" You need to ask questions; otherwise, your faith will become fake because God speaks in clear terms. He speaks.

When we say prayer is a channel of grace, it doesn't mean to pray repeatedly, "Father, give me grace. Give me grace." Most times, that's not what it is. If a person is accessing God through the channel of grace through worship, which we will explore in coming chapters, they wouldn't be singing songs like "God Give me grace" because they want grace. No, as you worship Him, grace will come regardless of whether the song is about grace. In the same way, if prayer is your channel of grace, it does not necessarily mean to pray repeatedly, "God give me grace." You've been doing that for a long time, but has the grace come?

Thank God for the Holy Spirit because He is the One that practically does the work in prayer, as seen in Romans 8:26-27, which says, *In the same way, the Spirit helps us in our weakness. We do not know what we ought to pray for, but the Spirit himself intercedes for us through wordless groans. And he who searches our hearts knows the mind of the Spirit because the Spirit intercedes for God's people in accordance with the will of God.* Over 90% of my personal prayers are in the spirit because regular prayer in your understanding can become incredibly monotonous. It would be extremely boring, especially if you don't want to go to vain repetition. Without the Holy Spirit, prayer would just be a futile exercise. I've learned that there's a direct relationship between praying in the Holy Spirit and faith because if you can pray in a language you don't understand but persist regardless, it will build your faith in believing what God's plan is for you that you haven't seen.

How many people feel like praying when they're down? Usually, this is when most people don't want to pray, but we can learn from Jesus, who had the Spirit of God without measure. In Matthew 26:36-46, when He was sorrowful because He was going to be crucified, He didn't become quiet about the sorrow; he prayed. Luke 22:44 mentions He prayed so much that His tears were like blood, meaning it wasn't a casual prayer. He really needed grace from His Father. In Matthew 14, when Jesus heard that His cousin John the Baptist, the person who baptized Him into ministry, was gruesomely murdered, he went up to the mountain to pray after feeding the multitude. Jesus knew He was getting emotionally drained because of the bad news, so He withdrew. It is often before your tires go out that you need grace. And if you're a well-trained driver, you would've realized long before that something was off somewhere. I heard a story of a person who kept driving their car for 30 minutes to their office and realized that something was wrong somewhere but paid no attention to it, only to find out when they arrived at the office that their tire was completely flat.

Jesus already knew He could not continue ministry with the bad news He heard. He needed to spend time praying to renew his strength;

otherwise, he would crash. When you see someone who has received bad news after losing a loved one and keeps going, they're just a disaster waiting to happen, and I feel for those people. They might seem like they're okay and everything is fine, but in many cases, it is just building up to the point of explosion. What you need in such situations is not consolation from people but to connect with God more than you have ever done because the devil will use that opportunity to steal, kill, and destroy. Many people come out of those things – if they ever come out – with their faith in God shaken already or punctured, and it's only a matter of time before you don't see them in God anymore because of offense. Jesus took time aside to recharge Himself through prayer and came back walking on water. The level of grace and faith in God had increased.

I can only imagine what Jesus was praying about, "Father, why was John the Baptist beheaded this week? Father, is this Your plan? Father, what are the next steps? What else do I need to do?" For Jesus, it was almost like a mentor died or was gruesomely murdered. John the Baptist was one of the first people to prophesy while He was an adult that "this is the Christ." In fact, Jesus' first few disciples were once disciples of John. The Bible says that immediately after John prophesied those words, his disciples just left and began following Jesus. And John was not offended because he knew that this was the Messiah.

We must know that there are times when prayer is what we must turn to, especially for those whose primary channel of grace is prayer. Some people can pray non-stop for six hours, believe it or not. They are prayer machines. If this is not your primary channel, you may be thinking right now, "how is it even possible?" But if worship is your primary channel of grace, you won't see it as a chore to worship for three hours. You wouldn't even realize you've been worshiping for that long. So, if you're still struggling with any of the channels, continue to hold on until you find your naturally gifted channel. That's the wisdom behind the message of the channels of grace.

I know of someone that prayed for three days straight. Now, remember, prayer is not just a one-way conversation. If that's what you think, you're probably already wondering, how can someone keep talking for three days non-stop? Like we said, prayer is communicating with God. Maybe you might talk for 30 minutes, and then God is responding to you for an hour. Hopefully, you're not speaking more than God. In the same way, people can meditate on the word and read the word for hours because God has naturally gifted them to be avid readers. So, we ought to locate our own channel of grace and use that to enter the presence of God. Once we have entered the Lord's presence, everything else will become easy.

Another situation where Jesus had to engage His channel of grace was in the garden of Gethsemane in Matthew 26:36-46,

Then Jesus came with them to a place called Gethsemane, and said to the disciples, "Sit here while I go and pray over there." And He took with Him Peter and the two sons of Zebedee, and He began to be sorrowful and deeply distressed. Then He said to them, "My soul is exceedingly sorrowful, even to death. Stay here and watch with Me." He went a little farther and fell on His face, and prayed, saying, "O My Father, if it is possible, let this cup pass from Me; nevertheless, not as I will, but as You will." Then He came to the disciples and found them sleeping, and said to Peter, "What! Could you not watch with Me for one hour? Watch and pray, lest you enter into temptation. The spirit indeed is willing, but the flesh is weak." Again, a second time, He went away and prayed, saying, "O My Father, if this cup cannot pass away from Me unless I drink it, Your will be done." And He came and found them asleep again, for their eyes were heavy. So He left them, went away again, and prayed the third time, saying the same words. Then He came to His disciples and said to them, "Are you still sleeping and resting? Behold, the hour is at hand, and the Son of Man is being betrayed into the hands of sinners. Rise, let us be going. See, My betrayer is at hand."

We are in this state sometimes, but many Christians push it aside. It's almost like it is a sin to acknowledge that we are feeling sorrowful. It's almost as if we feel guilty for feeling this way. The Bible says to rejoice with those rejoicing and mourn with those who are mourning. There is a time for everything. When Moses died, God allowed the children to mourn for 40 days, and after that, He said it was enough. He didn't scold them for mourning, but He also didn't allow them to go beyond the prescribed time. Jesus acknowledged His sorrow and was wise enough to tell those in His holies of holies, not any tom, dick and harry. The soul is weak, so when grace comes, it moves from God into your spirit and then into your flesh, which means the soul.

I want to ask you a question. Have you read anywhere in the Bible where Jesus sang praise or worship songs or asked for a minstrel to play instruments? David made many instruments, so in the time of Christ, there were instruments available, and people were singing. But almost every time, we see that Jesus always prayed. Every night, Jesus was praying. This is why some people concluded that prayer is the master key.

When God gave me this understanding of the channels of grace, it transformed my relationship with God. Jesus' primary channel of grace was prayer. The only time I know from my study of the gospels that Jesus worshiped was when He sent out His disciples, and they went out and came back, and the Bible said, *and He rejoiced in His heart* (Luke 10:21). That's the only thing that is close to worship. Other versions might have rendered it differently, but like the Bereans in Acts 17, study the scriptures to further your understanding.

Every time Jesus spent time in prayer, He got the result He wanted. If I do what He says needs to be done and I don't get results, I ask, "why is it not so?" I ask God questions, and He says, "have you considered this scripture?"

Some of us may not get those results through prayer but will get the same result Jesus got through worship because if you think about it, it is still communicating with God. Worship is not my primary channel of grace, so I have a list of worship songs that can take me to a place where I'm connected with God. I can remember songs from 15 years ago when I got into that zone. Even the channel of association is still communicating with God. Those who appear unto the Lord in Zion shall go from glory to glory. Basking in the presence of God is an avenue for connecting with God on different levels.

ANGELIC ASSISTANCE THROUGH PRAYER

Sometimes we are not communicating with God but with angelic beings. The Bible tells us in Hebrews 1:14 that certain ministering spirits are the servants of believers. Every child of God has angels assigned to them, and we can obtain grace by sending those ministering angels on errands; "ministering angels go before me and do this in Jesus' name."

PRAYER VS EXERCISING AUTHORITY

There are different ways we can pray. The Bible says in Mark 11:23 that if you tell this mountain to move, it will move. I don't consider that prayer, as I consider prayer to be communing with God. But there's another aspect which is exercising our authority. Sometimes we mix those two things. Let's take an example of a sick person who wants to be well, trusting God for healing. They will often go about it by praying, "Oh, God. I'm sick. I want You to heal me." But there's a point you'll get to in your understanding where you'll realize you don't have to take it to God because Jesus has already taken our infirmities according to Matthew 8:17, and by His stripes, we are healed (1 Peter

2:24). You'll begin to understand that you can just say to that sickness, "I rebuke you in the name of Jesus." Whether you see that as prayer or not is your choice, but I see that as exercising my authority because I am speaking to the mountain, not God. So, we can pray to the Father and exercise our authority by speaking to the things God has made.

COMMUNING WITH GOD

How can we pray so that God hears our prayers? Jesus gave us the model of prayer. The prayer that God will hear must be addressed to the Father and must end in the name of Jesus. That is the authorization. Using a letter as an example, for it to get delivered to the right place, it must have an address, and it must have a stamp for authorization. In the case of prayer, the address is the Father, and the stamp is the name of Jesus.

The spiritual realm from scripture is very disciplined. If you address a prayer to the Father, no demon has a right to intercept or take your prayer, as it were. The Bible makes it very clear that when you pray properly, it gets to God. That's why the Bible says if you ask your Father for bread, He will not give you stones. Now, the answers might be interrupted, like in Daniel's case. The Bible says in Daniel 10 that he prayed, then an angel came to him after 21 days and said, from the moment you prayed, God heard, but the angel bringing the response was hijacked by the prince of Persia and given to the king of Persia to hold in captivity. Within that name of Jesus, there are authorizations. A person who is not born again does not have the right to use the name of Jesus legally, except for the prayer of salvation, because the Bible says that God does not hear the prayer of sinners, that is, someone who sins as a lifestyle.

Communing with God must be a lifestyle thing. The Bible instructs us in 1 Thessalonians 5:17 to pray without ceasing, which means we ought to pray to God continuously and regularly. If you woke up in the morning, sent someone a text message, and started a conversation, you wouldn't expect the person to greet you again later, saying, "Hi." Some people do this and are incredibly formal, but most people would continue the conversation because they already said hi earlier that morning. When you start your day talking to God, you can just continue the conversation. Let me make it very clear. How we interact with the Father is different from how we interact with the Holy Spirit. Whenever we get a nudge to pray in a particular way, most times, it is because it is the Father that we are communing with at that time. In most cases, the Holy Spirit is the one that we can casually but not disrespectfully commune with, like a friend.

For example, when those three people that looked like men appeared to Abraham, they were not all Jesus but looked like men. We can also refer to when there was a fourth person in the fire with Shadrach, Meshach, and Abednego. Nebuchadnezzar said the fourth looked like the son of God. How did Nebuchadnezzar know how Jesus looked? All he was saying was that the fourth person looked like an angelic being not a human being. The Holy Spirit determines that kind of reverence for how we approach heavenly things. There are times I would be worshiping and know that I cannot be standing. There's a kind of presence that can be there, and I cannot remain standing because it would be highly disrespectful. I would know not to assume particular postures because I no longer feel comfortable. It's why sometimes when there is a visitation, and you don't quickly respond to what you're being nudged to do, the visitation leaves. While we're praying or worshiping, some of us know that we should be kneeling, but some of us get into our minds and wonder what people will think and if it's appropriate. Before you know what's happening, the visitation is gone, and you've lost an opportunity because the chief protocol officer told you that to receive something from God now, you must not be standing. That does not mean that every single time you pray, this is what you must do. We must be extremely sensitive to know when to switch gears. We don't take one way God has appeared to us and put it on a plaque and say, "this is the way." No, God is very dynamic.

One of the questions to reflect on is, "why am I communing with God?" Is it just for what I can get, or am I just fulfilling my duty? Why? I've said time and time again that the best experiences are the ones God Himself initiates. You're going about your daily duties, but suddenly you realize that God is knocking at the door of your heart, sometimes to say He loves you and then He goes away, as it were. But sometimes, you'll see that He's asking for your attention. For parents, have you ever been at work and the daycare, or the school called, and you had to leave work to go home? Do you tell them no because you're at work? No. So what's wrong with ending work early, just as if the child's daycare is calling because God wants to see you? Those are the most powerful experiences. When Moses came up to the mountain, it was God that requested for Him. We can seek God, but God can also seek us, and that's the better of the two. All we must do is respond. Revelation 3:20 says, *"Behold, I stand at the door, and I knock. If you open, I will come and I will dine with you."* I've found these to be the most notable experiences in my life, where I didn't really do anything, but all I had to do was respond.

In the earlier days of our marriage, my wife and I would have conversations where I'd be fully engaged, and then suddenly, I'd disengage, causing her to wonder if I was okay. Although I would tell her I was fine, it wasn't sitting well with her because it wasn't properly understood, so I had to communicate that to her. So now, if I disengage, she asks me if I'm receiving, and if I nod, I'm left alone. I tell you; these are the best experiences. If you can recognize His knock, respond to Him. This is the same as excusing yourself when you are in the middle of a conversation to pick up a phone call. Some people say it's rude in a conversation but lack understanding. If you can stop your conversation with someone to pick up the phone and don't see anything wrong with it, why do you feel bad when God calls your heart because it would be disrespectful to someone? Which one is ruder?

There are also instances where God can take sleep away from you because He wants to tell you something. Just like in the previous situation, if you're able to recognize what He is doing and you respond, you will enjoy it. There was a time I needed rest and was looking forward to sleeping, but I couldn't sleep. So, I got up, went to the family room, and started praying. After a bit, there was a period where I just kept quiet, and suddenly, I noticed that I had begun to travel. I was still in the family room, but I was traveling. Remember when Gehazi followed Naaman to pick up the goods from him, and he was lying to Elisha? And Elisha said, "Didn't my spirit go with you?" Elisha's body was there, but his spirit went with Gehazi. That's a good monitoring spirit. So, when Gehazi was lying, Elisha called him out on it. So going back to my encounter, I just saw myself moving until I arrived in Nigeria in a particular ministry. I was there at the altar, and a specific Pastor of that ministry laid hands on me, and I fell under the anointing. They picked me up, laid hands on me, and fell again. After that, I left, went to other places, and then came back into the Family Room and realized what had just happened. I had just had an encounter. I had that encounter not because I was seeking it in prayer but because God was the one who initiated it by taking my sleep from me. That's how I knew that, most likely, He was the one who initiated it. I could have forced myself to sleep or watched unprofitable things as many people do or could have just complained or maybe even taken some sleeping pills. We are spiritual people and therefore shouldn't walk like natural people. Some people even shared with me that they experienced someone tapping them to wake them up. The next time you feel like you can't sleep, wake up and spend time with God.

The Channel of Meditation

Be still, and know that I am God; I will be exalted among the nations, I will be exalted in the earth! The Lord of hosts is with us; the God of Jacob is our refuge. (Psalms 46:10-11)

The more valuable a thing is, the more effort people will make to create counterfeits. There are some currencies in the world that nobody would even try to counterfeit because the cost of counterfeiting them is more than the currency's value. I heard about a particular dollar in an African country that, at some point, to be able to buy a loaf of bread, you would have to put heaps of that currency in a wheelbarrow. Who is going to try and counterfeit that currency? It would be a waste of time. But you think about the Canadian dollar, the American dollar, or the British pound, and you see lots of effort to counterfeit them because of their value. Today, you'll see that there are so many attempts, and in some cases, successful attempts at counterfeiting meditation because of how valuable it is in the sight of God.

The Bible says in Psalms 46:10, *Be still and know that I am God.* If you are not still, then you will not know. The truth is, you can engage with every other channel of grace, but without understanding meditation, you might not be able to receive in your mind what God has released in your spirit.

What does it mean to "know"? It means to make sense of what you have gotten. Many of us have dreams and visions that we don't even understand, so it is of no value, just like the Ethiopian eunuch reading Isaiah 53 in Acts 8. The Holy Spirit had to send Philip to give him understanding because He knew he was confused. When Philip went to join him in the chariot, he asked, "do you understand what you're reading? The eunuch answered, "how can I understand if nobody teaches it to me and explains it to me?" See, without understanding, you're pretty much wasting your time. After he asked that question, Philip began to walk him through it, and his understanding became fruitful. Once his understanding was fruitful, he decided on his own to be baptized according to Acts 8:36, where he said, *"See, here is water. What hinders me from being baptized?"*

If you don't obey, you don't yet understand because there will be obedience wherever there is genuine understanding. For example, I don't drink pop anymore because I understand how dangerous it is to my body. Some people might have the information, but they don't yet have an understanding. Does anyone want to be sick or want their body to break down? Obviously not, but people have yet to connect information with the outcome, and that's what understanding does. It gets you to a point where people don't have to force you into making the right decisions. If you understand why you need to pick up the Word of God to read every day, even if it is one word, nobody would need to chase you around to study the Word. You have 24 hours in a day. Be still and know.

The devil's job is to steal, kill, and destroy. How does he do it? He's the master of deception. So many Christians are being deceived into something else and end up on one extreme or the other. On one end of the spectrum, we have people who avoid any form of meditation because they believe it simply means yoga, even though it is mentioned in the Bible over 30 times. People at the other end of the spectrum say there's nothing wrong with it because they're just "stretching." The stretching is not the problem. It is the goal of what they are doing that's the problem. If you are at a bus station, and the bus has a specific route number, but it has a different destination than where you want to go, why would you enter that bus? Yoga takes people to a different destination. Our destination is the presence of God. One of the side benefits is to quiet your mind, which is good, but what is entering your mind when it is quiet?

I want to ask you a rhetorical question, who taught you the smell of a stench? Who taught you the smell of a good scent? Did someone bring you an array of different smells to teach you? No! It is innate. That's why God put the nose close to the mouth so that when you are about to drink that spoiled milk, you can smell it and put it down. The Bible says in Romans 8:14 that, *for as many as are led by the Spirit of God, these are the sons of God.* When you are born again and spirit-filled, just as no one had to teach you what a stench smells like, no one teaches you, but it is rather the Holy Spirit leading you. Whether you know it or not is a different question entirely. We teach people how to identify and submit to the leading of the Holy Spirit, so they don't address Him as something, like some people say, "Something told me." That's like someone knowing your name, but they keep calling you by saying, "Hey, Something! Come here." We will not struggle to enter God's presence when we learn to access the throne of God through the natural strength He has given us.

Then Elijah said to Ahab, "Go up, eat and drink; for there is the sound of abundance of rain." So Ahab went up to eat and drink. And Elijah went up to the top of Carmel; then he bowed down on the ground, and put his face between his knees, and said to his servant, "Go up now, look toward the sea." So he went up and looked, and said, "There is nothing." And seven times he said, "Go again." Then it came to pass the seventh time, that he said, "There is a cloud, as small as a man's hand, rising out of the sea!" So he said, "Go up, say to Ahab, Prepare your chariot, and go down before the rain stops you.'" Now it happened in the meantime that the sky became black with clouds and wind, and there was a heavy rain. So Ahab rode away and went to Jezreel. Then the hand of the Lord came upon Elijah; and he girded up his loins and ran ahead of Ahab to the entrance of Jezreel. (1 Kings 18:41-46)

Elijah was one person among many in scripture that operated in the channel of meditation. In verse 43, the servant kept going and coming back to Elijah because Elijah was meditating. In this passage, the Bible does not mention that he prayed, but he was still receiving from the supernatural; how? There is time for everything under the sun, as mentioned in Ecclesiastes 3. There are times I go to God having a lot to say, and I sense the Holy Ghost telling me to keep quiet. There is a time to talk and a time to be quiet, a time to worship and a time to be quiet, a time to pray and a time to be quiet, a time to read the word and a time to cease reading the word because God wants to speak to you. We need to be sensitive to timing.

If you can visualize Elijah's posture in this scripture, you'll probably be able to connect it to some of the meditation postures in the world today. Many believers have shied away from it due to the name(s) they are called, such as yoga, etc. Habakkuk 2:1 shows us another meditation posture; *I will stand my watch and set myself on the rampart and watch to see what He will say to me, and what I will answer when I am corrected.* In essence when we are meditating, we are waiting to see, hear, and perceive. That is the art of meditation, waiting to receive what God, perhaps, has to say to us.

Now, what does it mean to be quiet in God's presence? It means to focus your mind and your thoughts on God. If I asked you to meditate on a physical object, you would be able to focus your mind on it because it is tangible, and you can see it. How can you meditate on something and someone that you cannot see? How can you focus on God you cannot see? Focus on the things that represent God. For example, some of us know the scent that some of our close ones have, so the moment you smell that scent, you know that person is around. Perhaps, even having access to something that belongs to them can remind you of them. Even their pictures, messages or anything connected to them can remind you of them. So, when we say to be quiet in God's presence, it means to wait on God, meditate on who He is and His ways, and the Holy Ghost will lead you, accordingly, depending on what is needed at that point in time. I'll explain them below.

WAIT SILENTLY ON GOD

Habakkuk 2:20 says, *"But the Lord is in His holy temple. Let all the earth keep silence before Him."* The first step is to be completely silent, not thinking about anything but simply waiting to hear, perceive, or for divine connection. When someone tells you they're coming to visit you and gives you a specific time, even while doing something else, your mind is at the door waiting for their arrival. You suspect that any little sound you hear is their arrival because you know they're coming.

Zephaniah 1:7 says, *Be silent in the presence of the Lord God; For the day of the Lord is at hand, For the Lord has prepared a sacrifice; He has invited His guests.* I was once in court supporting someone and was able to observe the protocol in that place. You dare not utter a word except if you're called upon to speak; otherwise, you'll be in contempt of the court. Everywhere was silent, and I thought, "wow, this is what it means to be silent in the presence of God." When you begin to practice this, it could be a little challenging because, for some of us, our minds keep moving from one thought to another but don't lose heart. We don't do what is easy, but we do what is right until it becomes easy. Sit down quietly and hold your thoughts, and gradually you'll begin to get a hold of them. It's good when you start by silencing the environment around you, but the deeper you go, even though things are noisy around you, you'll be able to be quiet on the inside to know when His still, small voice is speaking.

Some people don't know when they've offended God. One of the ways that people offend God without knowing is through their carnal chatter. They're unaware that God is in the place, and they need to be quiet. And this is something that some denominational churches, like the Catholic church, have built a system around. They train the people to assume a particular posture once they enter the church. We might not understand what they've chosen to do, but we need to understand that there's a certain reverence we must accord God when in his presence, especially if we want it to remain.

If you have read the book, "5 Hindrances to Growth in Grace" by Kenneth E Hagin, you'll see it mentioned there. I see the way some people talk loosely, not even being aware of their environment. They say God is not talking to them, though they disrespect His presence. If I am in the presence of God and someone is talking to me, sometimes I'll have to ignore them to maintain my communion with God. I can later apologize to a person for ignoring them but the cost of missing a timely word from God can be grave. We must understand these things and be our brother's keeper. There are times when the Word of God is moving very powerfully, and you can sense the spirit of God moving during worship or announcements. That's not the time to make side comments and have side conversations. Some people might be having visitations that you are unaware of. That unnecessary comment can cause their divine visitation to end. They were in the spirit, enjoying their encounter, and now they've come back to the earthly realm because of your interruption.

MEDITATE ON WHO GOD IS

The second way to meditate is on the person of God. Psalm 145:5, reads, *I will meditate on the glorious splendor of Your majesty And on Your wondrous works.* What does this mean? It means meditating on the characteristics, the nature of God, and the love of God. Some of us may have experienced this, but you may not have known what you were experiencing. You were meditating, and suddenly, His love and faithfulness just started overshadowing you. Generally, this is one of the paths toward growing in love with anything. The more you set your eyes on it, the more your affection grows for it. The Bible says we should flee every appearance of evil because the more we meditate on evil, the more we are drawn to it. Meditate on the nature and characteristics of God and the splendor of His majesty. The picture of the way heaven is and the throne room of God. If God has ever given you a picture of the throne room, meditate on it, this is a good way to access Him. Do not imagine things on your own. Let God be the one to supply it to you, and when He does, hold on to it.

MEDITATE ON THE ACTS OF GOD

Finally, we can meditate on God's acts. Looking at the same scripture as above, Psalms 145:5, His acts represent His wondrous works. What has He done for you? Do you remember the way He brought you out of that impossible situation? That's why we must have a book of remembrance to which we can always refer. I am not just talking about sleeping and waking up because that's thanksgiving. I'm talking about testimonies. When you didn't know how that bill was going to get paid and someone called you without knowing your situation and said, "God sent me to you," then sent the exact amount of money needed and just moved you to tears. Or meditate on how that word of prophecy came to you accurately when you needed it the most. The times God saw you through your school and provided for your tuition and how God connected you with your destiny helper. Or when you were sick, and the Holy Ghost reminded you that you have anointing oil and told you to pick it up and anoint yourself. And you immediately dragged yourself there, anointed yourself, went to sleep, and woke up the next morning as if you were never sick. What do you think will happen when next, God forbid, the enemy tries to attack your body, your finances or even attempts to harbor offense with your helper of destiny? Meditate on that same testimony and remember the amazing acts of God.

Many of us have anointing oil in our homes, unused sitting as decor, while others get results daily from using it. Someone shared with me that they were experiencing certain symptoms and applied the oil with some other creams. The sickness left, but she was unsure whether it was the cream or the anointing oil that cured it. The next time, she used the oil by itself, and immediately, the pain went away. These are a few of God's works, and we can go on and on and on because what God cannot do does not exist. Sometimes the problem with us is that we remember issues more than we remember testimonies. Do you know that God instructed the Israelites to continually meditate on how He brought their fathers out of Egypt? On how He brought the plague upon the Egyptians? He instructed that they must never forget. So, testimonies don't have expiry dates. Or rather, they shouldn't. Psalms 77:12 says, *I will also meditate on all Your work, and talk of Your deeds.* Make this your usual practice. When you face challenges, meditate on your past victories. Light and darkness cannot cohabit in the same place.

When Saul doubted David's ability to fight against the Philistine Goliath, David told him the same God that saved me from the lion and bear would deliver me from the hand of this Philistine in 1 Samuel 17:37. He didn't forget. As a matter of fact, he used that same testimony to give Him confidence that the same God who did it for him before can do it again. As you meditate on those victories, you will feel the same energy you felt in that moment. Don't replay how someone offended you because you will feel the same pain of offense, which can never take you to a place of strength.

MEDITATION AIDS

1. **Worship**: This is one of the tools that can aid your meditation, a song can only take you to where it came from, so we must choose these songs carefully. A worship song that did not come from God will not take you to God. Some songs sound good, and the lyrics are good, but it's just the flesh that it's activating. I prefer instrumentals, songs with no words because sometimes the words can be very distracting. I find in many cases that once the worship takes you to that place in God, you might have to turn off the music, so we need to be sensitive to that.
2. **Quiet Environment**: Try to quiet your environment as much as possible. You can limit distractions by doing things such as

using headphones to suppress the noise around you or putting your phone on airplane mode
3. **Maintain a comfortable position**: Your body can talk to you too and if there is pain, this can be a distraction. Some people have to sit down with their legs outstretched to have good blood flow. You can also adopt Elijah's posture (see 1 Kings 18:42). But whatever position you choose, ensure it won't make you sleep.

The Channel of Worship

"But the hour is coming, and now is, when the true worshipers will worship the Father in spirit and truth; for the Father is seeking such to worship Him." (John 4:23)

I left the grace channel of worship till the end because many people already know this channel, but we should still investigate it. One of the best ways to learn how to approach God is by learning from those God has naturally gifted to approach Him, that is, the prophets. The prophetic can be triggered through music, which we see in many instances throughout the Bible. Look at 1 Samuel 10:5-6,

After that, you shall come to the hill of God where the Philistine garrison is. And it will happen, when you have come there to the city, that you will meet a group of prophets coming down from the high place with a stringed instrument, a tambourine, a flute, and a harp before them; and they will be prophesying. Then the Spirit of the Lord will come upon you, and you will prophesy with them and be turned into another man.

Before we get into this scripture, let's look at it from a natural standpoint. We understand that we can use our phones to call someone in another country and engage in a conversation. There are no wires between us and them because the words are going through the atmosphere in sound waves using different kinds of equipment such as receivers and transmitters that do different things to move these words. In IT security, it is called a "man in the middle attack," where someone can inject themselves in the middle of a conversation between two parties to intercept their messages. When they do this, it gives them the ability to change the messages in real-time. That is the natural realm.

In the spiritual realm, words are also moving around, and worship is a mode of transportation to move us to the place where the words we need to hear are travelling. This is what the scripture is explaining, and to a large extent, that is what discernment means. Notice in that same 1 Samuel 10:5-6 that the Holy Spirit came upon them, and they knew what to prophesy after they engaged with the instruments. The prophetic is easy when we understand what to do, and the route to it is in these channels of grace. Every word that we need is on the earth somehow, and if it's not there, it can be brought to the earth if we know what to do.

We also see the same in 2 Kings 3:1-15, when Elisha said, *"bring me a minstrel."* If you read this passage, you'll see that Elisha was offended by some of the kings there, and so he couldn't hear from the Lord, hence calling for a minstrel for assistance. Who is a minstrel? An instrumentalist or a singer. As the minstrel was playing, the word of God came. Verse 15 of this passage says, *"But now bring me a musician." Then it happened, when the musician played, that the hand of the Lord came upon him.* Meaning that music can be a tool to connect with divinity.

In the days of Saul, the people knew when Saul was under demonic oppression and knew what the king needed was grace through music. Most likely, Saul's channel of grace was music because, without fail, he always received grace through this channel. Look at 1 Samuel 16:14-23:

But the Spirit of the Lord departed from Saul, and a distressing spirit from the Lord troubled him. And Saul's servants said to him, "Surely, a distressing spirit from God is troubling you. Let our master now command your servants, who are before you, to seek out a man who is a skillful player on the harp. And it shall be that he will play it with his hand when the distressing spirit from God is upon you, and you shall be well." So Saul said to his servants, "Provide me now a man who can play well, and bring him to me." Then one of the servants answered and said, "Look, I have seen a son of Jesse the Bethlehemite, who is skillful in playing, a mighty man of valor, a man of war, prudent in speech, and a handsome person; and the Lord is with him." Therefore Saul sent messengers to Jesse, and said, "Send me your son David, who is with the sheep." And Jesse took a donkey loaded with bread, a skin of wine, and a young goat, and sent them by his son David to Saul. So David came to Saul and stood before him. And he loved him greatly, and he became his armor bearer. Then Saul sent to Jesse, saying, "Please let David stand before me, for he has found favor in my sight." And so it was, whenever the spirit from God was upon Saul, that David would take a harp and play it with his hand. Then Saul would become refreshed and well, and the distressing spirit would depart from him.

Do you see how specific the request for a minstrel was? Out of all the instruments, why did they request a harp? They realized that something happened to him every time he heard the harp play. These channels are about knowing yourself. What do you know about yourself? What instrument or song gets you connected regardless of the situation? Here it's specifically the harp, but when we say music, it can be words, the piano, guitar, drums, trumpet, the sax, tambourine, flute, or something else. It can have a slow or a fast tempo and sometimes even a combination of some of these things. We need to be sensitive. Study yourself, date yourself, and be sensitive to what easily gets you connected to God. You must explore these things in many cases, as they will not just be handed to you. Growing with God is an adventure.

Having no music is better than having bad music. Skill is needed when it has to do with this channel of grace; otherwise, there would be no strength flowing from the channel. A person can be connected and suddenly become disconnected because of one misplayed key. The music needs to be sung and played well. It's not about having numerous lyrics either. Many times, you only need the chorus replaying repeatedly. It sounds simple, but there is power in it. If your primary channel is worship and you connect with ungodly music, you are exposing yourself to disaster. You would never be able to hear clearly from God. Never. Because you're polluted. That's why the devil will keep encouraging you to keep listening to that kind of music. Jesus came and died on the cross for you. Is it too much for Him to ask you to give up certain types of music?

For worship to be effective, certain conditions must be met. In teaching the Samaritan woman, Jesus Christ exposed us to a critical component of worship that will get God's attention. In John 4:21-24, Jesus corrected the assertion that our Heavenly Father must be worshiped in a particular geographical location to show up. Instead, Jesus said that we are now at a time when our Heavenly Father will only require spirit-led and truthful worship to make an appearance. Additionally, Jesus also said that when we worship in spirit and truth, the Father will look for us. Now you might be wondering what worship in spirit and in truth means. Let me explain.

Spirit-led worship is one that the Holy Spirit inspires. Worship that will be acceptable to God is one that edifies the spirit, not the flesh. There is music that stimulates the flesh and worldly desires and does not cause us to hallow God in our hearts. On the other hand, there is music that, from the moment you listen to it, you are encouraged to contemplate about God. Spirit-led worship is atmosphere-changing worship. Do you know that some so-called gospel songs are danced to in clubs? Yes, absolutely! Unfortunately, some gospel artists are more concerned about winning Grammys than communicating the mind of Jesus Christ to the people of God.

Worshiping in truth is a matter of your heart and disposition to the song you are listening to. It is about interacting with worship sincerely and from a place of integrity. For example, you are singing the song, "I lift my hands to the great I Am," yet you are not lifting your hands. If the song talks about kneeling and you are singing the song, are you kneeling? This might seem like a minor thing but will have profound implications. Can you imagine someone saying they are at home while they are out and about? In speaking about integrity, Jesus profoundly said, *"But let your 'Yes' be 'Yes,' and your 'No,' 'No."* For whatever is more than these is from the evil one (Matthew 5:37). Jesus also took on the hypocrites of His day when He said, *"These people draw near to Me with their mouth, and honor Me with their lips, but their heart is far from Me"* (Matthew 15:8).

If worship is your channel of grace, you will realize that music moves you deeply. You don't need to know how to sing, but you draw strength from interaction with music. Listen to gospel songs, keep track of those you connect deeply with, and use them in your worship experience.

Remember that the essence of the channels of grace revelation is to enhance your ability to connect with God. God has uniquely gifted us to enable us to connect with Him without effort. The evidence of grace is the absence of stress. If you are still operating with stress, I pray that you receive grace through this book in Jesus' name.

4

Impartation of Grace

Many people are in need because they don't know what they need. When Solomon had an encounter with the Lord, The Lord asked Him what do you want in the dream? He didn't say he wanted a million dollars, as that is shallow thinking. There is a level where you'll think a million is a lot of money until you buy a house that is 700,000 dollars. But Solomon asked for wisdom to lead God's people. I want to be able to add value to people's lives. If I keep adding value to people's lives, value will also return to me. It makes no sense to ask God for material things. Ask Him for grace to add value to people's lives, and you'll never be dispensable. David, in a way, made himself indispensable because of the amount of value he was adding. According to Psalms 78:72, David did this by leading by the integrity of his heart and the skillfulness of his hands.

Why don't people storm out of the doctor's office angrily after waiting for an hour? You had an appointment for 1 pm, and they just took you to rooms to wait. Why didn't you leave in anger? It's because of the value. Ask, "Lord, give me the grace to add value to people's lives."

Paul said in 1 Corinthians 15:10, *But by the grace of God I am what I am, and His grace toward me was not in vain; but I labored more abundantly than they all, yet not I, but the grace of God which was with me.* After he received grace, he was able to labour more than them all. Labour is sweet when you're operating under grace. How frustrating is it for a student to read something for 6 hours without remembering or understanding anything? But when the grace is flowing, that same student will enjoy studying.

I was in Bible school, and a particular minister told me it takes him about twenty hours to prepare one sermon. The question in my head was, "what would happen for two services or three services?" If you don't know how to access grace, the struggle will continue. Grace is what eases pain, shame, and stress in a person's life. When grace is at your disposal, help will be available to you. When you are operating under grace, it will look as if you're not doing anything. For instance, it's funny how they say certain past American Presidents are good speakers when other people write their speeches. They were who they were by the help they received. When you receive help, you look like a superstar. The helper is behind the scenes, and He puts you like the show person to stand in front.

We all have 365 days in a year, yet not everybody can point to something definite other than waking up, eating, and sleeping that they achieved that year. It's painful to go through the entire year and have nothing extraordinary to show for it. If you're in that category, the Lord sees your pain; what you need is grace, then the labor will come after the grace has been released. I pray that the God of grace may visit you.

A yearning in my spirit is what Paul told the church in Romans 1:11-12, which reads, *For I long to see you, that I may impart to you some spiritual gift, so that you may be established— that is, that I may be encouraged together with you by the mutual faith both of you and me.* This is God's heart towards you, as He longs to see you established.

Without the gift, there will be no establishment. Let's assume you want to build a house. You'll need heavy equipment like bulldozers to clear the ground so that the land can be utilized. The gifts, in this case, are bulldozers to clear the ground so we may be established and be able to take dominion. They say if wishes were horses, even beggars would ride. The gift moves us from wishing to acting. It pushes us forward. I see many people sit down with desires, "I want to do this, I want to do that," but they are unable to do it. What they need are the gifts of the spirit. We don't go to places or get things done through our strength. Take inventory of what God can supply to you. Every good gift comes from above, and God can give them to you.

Now, this is the mystery, in the body of Christ, the grace flows from the top. We understand this in Psalms 133:1-2, which says, *Behold, how good and how pleasant it is for brethren to dwell together in unity! It is like the precious oil upon the head, running down on the beard, The beard of Aaron, Running down on the edge of his garments.* Unity here refers to the unity of giftings, unity of visions; everybody is succeeding. Not that some are up, and some are down, and you're questioning if some are even part of the family. A lion in Africa is still a lion in Canada. God only ever created fully grown trees, animals, and humans in the beginning. Since then, God has been hiding trees inside seeds, men and women inside babies, lions inside cubs, etc.

When God wants to start something, He calls a person and gives them grace with the intention of its replication. When you look at children, you are not surprised that they look like their father and mother.

When grace comes upon you, and you just find yourself desiring to add value and doing so consistently, people may look at you and say you're hardworking, but it's just the grace at work. Ordinary people get tired, yet some will keep on going and going. Grace! For instance, it took grace for planes to begin to fly, but they eventually realized they didn't want to waste time landing fighter jets to refuel. So why not refuel in the air so the mission does not get disrupted? Now they are working on turning air into fuel for fighter jets, so they are charging as they are moving. This is what I desire for myself too.

There is also a company in Germany that is making solar panel cars to achieve the same goal as the fighter jets. While normal people are driving, they park to refuel when their fuel becomes depleted or park to recharge in the case of electric vehicles before they move on, while others are charging while they are moving. Imagine having a race between these three vehicles. You may think you're competing with them until you realize they don't have to stop to charge or refuel. Just as each of these cars is on different levels, so are there different levels of grace. But as you move, grace can be recharged continually, just as the solar panelled car.

God desires that you not only see people that are moving in grace, but you will also become a replication of grace, for grace to become your identity. As you continue to read, I advise you to identify stress areas and begin to trust God for grace in those areas. Don't make excuses for mistakes; find out the grace you're lacking. If you get angry too much because of human beings, you need the grace to love people because people are people everywhere. You think if everybody were like you, the world would be a better place. No. In fact, you possibly irritate people and perhaps they just haven't told you yet. Everyone irritates someone else. It takes the grace of God to look at people, love them and see why they are doing things the way they are doing them.

Evidence of Grace

WISDOM

It takes wisdom to be able to arrange God's plans and purpose to come to fulfillment on the earth. It takes wisdom to run, not be weary, and go up consistently. It takes wisdom for things to work the way they should. The labour of fools wearies them, for they don't know how to get to where they are going according to Ecclesiastes 10:15, but when there is wisdom, you know how to get your desires met. If you desire a promotion, wisdom will cause you to know exactly when to request that promotion and the exact steps to take to receive it.

Wisdom is the ability to apply the Word to get results, not just quoting the Word. When there is wisdom, everything works: the output also increases as the grace increases. For example, marriage is an example of something that works by wisdom. It is common sense to know that two people can't be fighting at the same time. Imagine if you were walking along the street and a mad person came to you saying, "excuse, excuse me," would you attend to them? No. It is wisdom to know we don't listen to the devil's suggestions because he is a mad man. Knowing where God has put you and staying in that lane is wisdom. Nobody likes to fail, yet people take themselves out of their area of strength to prove a point and keep making mistakes.

POWER

Power is the ability to get things done. When you set a goal, wisdom will help you plan, but power will help you implement the plan. Wisdom will help you know the steps to take according to your destination, but power will help you take those steps daily whether you feel like it or not or if you feel anointed or not. Sometimes you must push your way through, and it takes power to do that. You need the power to take charge of your mind. A powerful book to read to dominate your mind is "Battlefield of the Mind" by Joyce Meyer. If God sends a word and the mind sends another word, which one would you believe? When there is power, you can command your mind to believe all that God has said to you. It takes power to say, "no, this word must come to pass," and God can give you that power.

The heart of man is deep, so for you to be able to hear or read the word and be convicted and remember the word the next day, it took power to drive it through every hindrance till it got into your heart and soul. Do you realize the number of things people get exposed to? Do you know how much information you've exposed yourself to just by scrolling on your phone for 5 minutes? Yet the word still powered through all those things.

Someone said to me she had an encounter with the Holy Spirit where her body was vibrating just by listening to my album "Divine Encounter."

God has made power available, so you cannot be weak. It's time to say, "Satan, I will no longer be a pushover." It takes power to move through obstacles and pain and still be able to move forward. This world does not respond to weakness. Let's look at Micah 3:8. *But truly I am full of power by the Spirit of the Lord, and of justice and might, to declare to Jacob his transgression and to Israel his sin.* Do you see why many people cannot confront situations? It takes power. It takes power to say, "Satan, this is the last time you come into this house; I am seated in heavenly places, and where a king is that's his kingdom; you don't step into this place. These children don't belong to you, don't come here again in the mighty name of Jesus!" It takes power to touch your body to say, "Pain, I command you to leave now in the name of Jesus." The word is in your mouth.

Everyone that is a child of God has access to grace. Let me tell you something, it is not reading that gives understanding or comprehension; it is grace. Readers are leaders, amen, but pick up the book and begin to read. It is one thing to read and another to understand what you're reading. The Ethiopian eunuch was reading but was not understanding what he was reading until Philip the Evangelist came to expound the scripture.

I don't know about others, but in my case, I'll be going about my duties, and the Holy Spirit will be explaining scripture. That is the grace the Holy Spirit gives. To teach the word, yes, there is a part you must play in reading the Bible, but most of it is played by the Holy Spirit. It's not about how many articles you read or powerful messages you listen to, it's about the Holy Spirit giving you understanding, and I knew when that grace came. Before then, I would look at the Bible but would not understand much from it. I'll memorize scripture without understanding, but suddenly, I began to see things in the Word of God one day. I tell you; grace is readily available to every child of God.

VISION

Vision is the ability to see. To be short-sighted is a defect. In Ecclesiastes 2:24, Solomon missed his way and said, "let us eat today for tomorrow we die," and he had no plan for the future whatsoever.

Vision is the ability to live in the now while still planning for the future. Only those who plan for the future will take charge of the future. Do you have an idea of what will or should happen in your life ten years from now? Do you know that life events happen in waves or patterns? While people are still living in the past, there are waves being created today. You might have missed out on a previous pattern but get ready for the next wave of blessings and opportunities coming your way in Jesus' name. Planning for the future while living in and navigating today takes vision. So, when making a decision, we should be thinking, "will this thing still be valid five or ten years from now?" If it is not going to be valuable, then we should not be investing time in it. But some people cannot genuinely see beyond one week; six months is too much, and let's not even talk about one year from now. But God will open your eyes today.

Vision is the ability to see the future and plan for the future you have seen. It is the ability to know what you want tomorrow and begin to live your life today in preparation for that tomorrow. If you tell people to start to plan for the next ten years, some people will think it is so far away as if it will never come. But the truth is, ten years is very close.

DISCIPLINE

What is discipline? The ability to subdue your flesh to pursue or attain a particular goal. The Bible says in Ecclesiastes 10:18 that through idleness of hands, the building decays. Discipline is something God makes available to a person. It's not enough to have one great performance. But when you see consistency, you know discipline is at work behind the scenes. You can never have consistency without discipline. Nobody wants to be the one that was once shining. I don't know about you, but I want to be in the now, not what once was. But this takes discipline. It takes discipline to say, "today I am walking with God, whether I feel like it or not" and then you start moving or saying, "today I will begin to serve whether I like it or not." It takes discipline to keep getting results day after day. When I wake up, I don't check my feelings to decide whether I am going to preach or not. Be the one to tell your body what to do, "when I say go, you go, when I say stop, you stop."

Someone said discipline is the soul of an army. I've realized that one person can have one gift and excel because of discipline while another can have multiple gifts and still be a failure because of a lack of discipline. Can you imagine a military that lacks discipline? I wouldn't want to be in such a country.

If you're struggling in this area, make it your desire to receive this grace. When you are disciplined, you'll become a hot cake. You'll be wanted everywhere by everyone. I used to love to sleep so much, but now one of my prayers is to operate without food and sleep if I can, without any negative reactions.

RICHES

The ability to get wealth. I'm telling you now to refuse to be broke. Don't even entertain the thought of it. A family shared with me how they became millionaires. They were doing their regular nine to five until they heard a word that recalibrated their thinking. They began to have desires, and God began to open doors. Within 2 years, they had 6 houses. Now they are employers of labour.

JOY

Everyone goes through challenges, but not everyone sees challenges the same. When you allow joy in your life, your perspective of challenges will be different. Some new people at our church genuinely believed we were faking our joyful nature until they repeatedly came and realized that we were not pretending.

You'll hear some people's stories and wouldn't even know they were going through the situations they went through, had they not told you. So, we don't wait for everything to be fine before we become joyful. It starts now. It takes grace. Out of your belly shall flow rivers of living waters, and joy is one of the rivers. You'll wake up every day with joy. Joy unspeakable! There are some people you'll meet and think they crucified Jesus. If you're focusing on problems, you'll always feel heavy, but when you focus on Jesus, you'll notice your problems demolished, and you'll be lifted from glory to glory. Receive joy in the name of Jesus!

LEADERSHIP

The ability to take the lead. A member of the church who attends a Christian school shared a testimony of how they were given an assignment, "How to Poop on Jesus," that she refused to do. According to the testifier, students were offered the assignment year after year, yet many casual Christians were still doing it. How can you be a Christian attending a Christian school and allow the professor to give you an assignment that bashes Jesus' name and not say anything? It takes the grace of leadership to stand up for such things. Many Christians knew it was not right but were too weak to stand up. The same problem occurs in music schools, where many Christians are forced to sing songs that they don't want to sing. But it's only those with the leadership grace that can boldly say that they want a clean band.

You see, when a leader is present, there is no complaining. When you find people who complain, you find people who lack leadership grace. If you can change it, why are you complaining? Fix it. The leadership grace is a fixing grace. We fix problems and don't repeat problems. Stop complaining and start leading.

When you look at a small nation like Israel and see that they have way more noble arrests than any other country, including those countries with high populations like China and India, you know there is a leadership grace.

FAITH

When we moved into our first church building amid the Covid-19 pandemic, the Lord instructed us to start a second service, and I am pleased to tell you that we started that second service. And we were not speaking to empty chairs either! It would have been easy to hear this from God when the first service was overflowing with people, but God decides the way He wants to do what He wants to do. Faith is the ability to believe in God. Even when you don't want to believe, you'll still find yourself believing. So, when He says to take a step, and you don't see the step or a bridge, but He is saying take it anyway, you're able to believe and take the step. This is when you'll now begin to see the step appearing.

PERSEVERANCE

Perseverance is the ability not to give up. I said earlier that if wishes were horses, even beggars would ride. I've realized something - there are times when God just says to go. He didn't say you'll succeed, but He said go to test you. He said concerning the Israelites, "I allowed them to go around in the wilderness that I may test their heart." Is that not wickedness? No, it is not. When you pass the test, it's promotion time afterward. Look at Joseph; he was there until the word of God found him, and it tested him. It is easy to love God when everything is working, but what happens when He allows things not to work when you're in a controlled environment? It is called a test. But perseverance is the ability to say, "no, I am here. Come rain or shine; I am here." It's not just mere talk; the Holy Ghost powers it.

You are showing up even when you don't feel like showing up. Do you think it was easy for Elisha to walk with Elijah when he wanted to get the double portion? It took perseverance. Elijah told him to leave multiple times, but he persisted. There is a trait that people call grit, and I've realized that this trait is not popular anymore because of pleasure. It's as if people are becoming weaker and giving up quicker. Things have become easier now, so any minor inconvenience and people say, "I'm done, I give up." Have you ever asked yourself, "what next after I give up?" Perseverance is that ability to never let those words come out of your mouth because you'll just find yourself holding on come rain, come shine.

Do you know what it took for Abraham to wait 25 years for Isaac? Perseverance. Do you know what it took for the woman who had an issue of blood for 12 years to be healed? She had this condition for 12 years, yet she still had faith to say, 'I'll try again. I've been to every physician and pharmacist you can think of, but if only I may touch, I know I will be made well.' That is perseverance, not giving up. It means not giving up on relationships, people, your dreams, or the vision God has given you. No vision begins to manifest from day one. Anybody telling you that is either ignorant or is just deceiving you. Even Jesus didn't begin to manifest His glory from the moment He was born, according to John 2:11. Continue to hold on till the very end, let others give up, but decide that you won't give up.

While I was a youth pastor, I used to look for every excuse to meet with my pastor to cancel the youth service. If the rain were too hard, I'd tell him, "Pastor, it's raining really, hard. I don't think the youth will be able to make it to youth church." and he would say, "Pastor Emmanuel, whether it rains, whether it snows, whether the sun is shining, we are going to have youth service." I would then ask, "what if nobody comes?" and his reply was always, "if nobody comes, it will just be you and the youth leaders. No matter what, we'll have youth service." And to this very day, that is still that same spirit that I carry. No matter what happens, there will be a service so long as there's a way. No one calls or messages me asking whether there will be a service or not. I pray God will give us grace.

Why do people need confirmation after confirmation? It's because of a lack of perseverance. You may have forgotten, but God has an excellent memory and knows what He said. You need to confirm again because you are about to give up. If everything were going well, you wouldn't need multiple confirmations. When you receive the grace to persevere, you will no longer need unnecessary confirmation again because you know it shall be once He has said it. Once has He spoken, twice have you heard. All power belongs to God. If God wants to change His mind, He will tell you. Just move with what He has said.

And please keep in mind that these giftings are not to show you how deficient you are but show you how much of God you need. As you read this, God will minister to you.

I'll give you an example. One of the church members was well qualified in his field, but for whatever reason, he was not receiving job offers where he believed he was supposed to be. Since he has a young family, after many months and then a year as his Pastor, it got to a point where I told him, "I think you should take the offers that are coming from out of town; because a man that cannot take care of his family is worse than an infidel (1 Timothy 5:8)." He replied, "with all due respect, God has put me here, and He has not told me that He is taking me somewhere else." I advised him that his family could remain in Edmonton, and he could travel back and forth. He replied, "Pastor, the truth is, I don't believe God is moving me." Another year went by, then five months before he landed a job, and now he is going from glory to glory. Perseverance is a major key to enjoying the best that God has to offer His children! Therefore Hebrews 6:12 instructs us to persevere as we seek to inherit God's promises.

Before God can trust you with something, He will test you with something. God can bring everything He has said to you to pass. Even if it will take ten years, keep on waiting. That is what perseverance is and is what Abraham clearly displayed. Abraham is our father, so we have access to the giftings and the grace of God upon his life. Ask yourself the question, "do I give up too quickly? Do I see challenges and turn away from them?" If so, it means you lack perseverance. Take it to God and tell Him that you desire perseverance.

THE SPIRIT OF BOLDNESS

Some people are too timid and afraid. They talk like no tomorrow in their rooms, but when they come out, they are mute. You need boldness to open your mouth. There are many things moving in your mind, but the ability to speak comes from God. Some people can't even maintain eye contact.

Micah 3:8 says, *But truly I am full of power by the Spirit of the Lord, and of justice and might, To declare to Jacob his transgression And to Israel his sin.* It takes boldness to be able to speak with authority. I don't mean shouting or being rude, but bold to stand your ground. Why can't many Christians live out their faith? It is because of peer pressure. What does peer pressure mean? They lack the boldness to take a stand. In church, they are screaming Hallelujah, but then amongst their friends, they can't shut down the world's request.

I remember working with a consulting company, and we went on a team lunch the day while I was on a Daniel fast. A Daniel fast involves maintaining a strictly vegan diet, including avoiding animal products, processed food, etc. I was like, "Lord should I go or not go, and how do I break the news to them?" There was a big emphasis on team bonding, so I was concerned about how my absence from the team lunch would have been viewed and what my prospect for promotion would be afterward. So, I decided to go with them, and coincidentally the restaurant didn't serve seafood, so I told them I wouldn't have any beef, and everyone looked at me, asking why? I now see why people faint in the face of challenges and opposition. In this instance, all eyes were on me the moment I asked not to be given meat. Folks, remember that it takes boldness to reign. Many people don't have any values because they always take the path of least resistance. It is often said that if you don't stand for something, you'll fall for anything. It takes boldness to take a stand.

Boldness is a virtue that can be transferred from one person to another. Many people have not yet tapped into boldness, so they still walk in timidity. They cannot confront a person when they offend them, so they live in offence while pretending to be fine. People observed the boldness that Peter and John displayed in Acts 4:13 and they exclaimed that it must have been imparted to them because of their association with Jesus Christ. May you be imparted with boldness as you read this book and follow the steps outlined for the transference of grace in Jesus' name.

HONOUR

In the first Samuel 10, Samuel met with Saul and said, "When you leave here, you'll meet some prophets who will hand over certain items to you." So, a portion of grace that Samuel operated in spilled on Saul, and he received a taste of what being honoured looked like. Therefore, honour is a grace that can be imparted from one person to another.

There is a grace for honour, and I'm not just talking about honour from men but from God. Let me tell you how you know God is honouring you:

1. **He gives you words in season (also known as revelation):** The Bible says in 1 Timothy 5:17, consider them double honor who labor in the Word and doctrine. So when God gives you a word in season, He is positioning you for double honor. The world will always pay attention to people armed with divine revelation. When what comes out of your mouth makes sense, you will be honored beyond your age. Likewise, when the words from a person's mouth make no sense, they will most likely be dishonored. In one instance, Jesus' teaching was so profound and life-changing that a woman blurted out from the crowd, *"Blessed is the womb that bore You, and the breasts which nursed You!"* (Luke 11:27).

2. **When He puts His glory on you:** I had an experience a few years ago when I went to a hospital to pray for a sick person. The security guard at the main entrance saw me and said, "I know you are a Pastor and a man of God, please pray for me." He immediately knelt down right there at the main entrance of the hospital where I prayed for him and left. When God puts His glory on you, regardless of your age, colour, or gender, you'll be honoured anywhere you go. Anyone that chooses to dishonour you will only do so at their own peril.

3. **When He puts His anointing on you**: When David ran away from Saul and heard Saul was coming after him, he ran to Samuel. Saul heard he was with Samuel, so he went after him. But the Bible says before he even got close to Samuel, Saul came under the anointing, tore his clothes, and began to prophesy like a mad man. When God puts His anointing on you, even crazy people will not deny that there is something about you. They might hate you and may never like you, but they can't do anything against you.
4. **He gives you wisdom.** Every time you see wisdom; you see honour. There is no way a person won't honour a wise man or woman. When you see the results of a person's life, the next thing that will come from your mouth is honour. Look how honourably Queen Sheba presented the gifts to Solomon (1 Kings 10:1-10).

Some people don't know what honour looks like and are too used to being disrespected. Someone shared a testimony with me that he went somewhere with someone, and something went missing. The people came accusing both of them of stealing it. He said he was shocked because he had never experienced something like that before. The Holy Spirit said to him, "don't you see the person you're with." Shame is transferable. You walk with honourable people, and you'll enjoy their honour. You walk with shameful people, and you'll share their disgrace. You cannot enjoy honour and move with dishonourable people because the shame upon them is transferable. And you can't blame God if you're partaking of the shame.

Joshua was a man that walked in divine honour. It was not possible to successfully take over from a prophet like Moses. The people heeded the instructions that Joshua gave them because of the honour upon Joshua. How did Joshua get that honour? The answer is in Numbers 27:18-20,

And the Lord said unto Moses, Take thee Joshua the son of Nun, a man in whom is the spirit, and lay thine hand upon him; And set him before Eleazar, the priest, and before all the congregation; and give him a charge in their sight. And thou shalt put some of thine honor upon him, that all the congregation of the children of Israel may be obedient."

God can impart you with honour through a person that carries the virtue.

What is Impartation?

Impartation is you receiving what someone else has worked to get. It is the release of grace from one vessel to another. Moses went on the mountain for 40 days twice. The Bible never told us Joshua did such a thing, yet he was able to do and finish the work Moses started.

Moses was one hundred and twenty years old when he died. His eyes were not dim nor his natural vigor diminished. And the children of Israel wept for Moses in the plains of Moab thirty days. So the days of weeping and mourning for Moses ended. Now Joshua the son of Nun was full of the spirit of wisdom, for Moses had laid his hands on him; so the children of Israel heeded him, and did as the Lord had commanded Moses. (Deuteronomy 34:7-9)

Joshua entered the labour of Moses through the laying of hands. The Lord said grace means somebody else has laboured, and you entered their labour and enjoyed its benefits. A good man leaves an inheritance. And not just material inheritance but also spiritual inheritances. What does that mean? The glory of the latter should be greater than the former. Someone once said, "I can see further because I stand on the shoulder of giants." Some people don't want to stand on anyone's shoulder, so they keep on toiling and toiling, reinventing the wheels of something already in existence. Instead of paying royalties for other people's patents, they won't stop until they've discovered their own.

Don't play games with your life. God has made grace available. The gift of God is without repentance, and you have a right to those gifts. You didn't pay your father or your mother to look like them. You were born the way you were because it is your right as their child. It is one of the reasons why the devil likes to separate people through rebellion and offence, so they don't have rights to anything.

The spirit of pride is an armed robber, and it robs people of what they can get through grace by making them do their own thing. Can you imagine Moses coming to lay hands for impartation on you and responding with no, you want to fast instead? That is what pride does to some people, and we must shut down these lies from the devil. If you take this approach, you'll never progress the way you ought to. Inheritance is available for you, so why start from scratch and not make any progress? We are to stand on the shoulders of giants so we can move further, which is why Joshua was able to finish what Moses didn't. He didn't start from the beginning but rather from where Moses ended.

So the Lord said to Moses: "Gather to Me seventy men of the elders of Israel, whom you know to be the elders of the people and officers over them; bring them to the tabernacle of meeting, that they may stand there with you. Then I will come down and talk with you there. I will take of the Spirit that is upon you and will put the same upon them; and they shall bear the burden of the people with you, that you may not bear it yourself alone." (Numbers 11:16-17)

It is one thing to have the Holy Spirit, but it's another thing to be mature enough to know how to engage with the Holy Spirit. Do you know there is a book on how to do Google searches? There is a way you'll search that only one result will appear. So, you can be baptized in the Holy Ghost, but it takes maturity to know the best way to maximally engage with the Holy Ghost. If a 3-year-old child engages with a Ph.D. holder in applied mathematics, the questions are limited to the child's understanding. But if you bring a person who has a master's in applied mathematics into the conversation, suddenly they can engage and draw more from that person. The little child is limited to asking about mundane things, yet there is exceeding grace available to the child. And for this reason, is why impartation is still relevant.

Impartation makes your spirit man mature quicker. It is like steroids in the spirit. That is what Jesus had. At the age of 12, He questioned the people in the sanctuary and asked them deep questions, way beyond what He could ordinarily do.

What Are The Qualifications?

We all know that not everyone is an ideal candidate for certain academic programs or jobs because of the requirements attached. Similarly, there are certain criteria that each person must meet for the release of grace, which means that not everyone is a candidate. So, what are the qualifications?

BE BORN AGAIN

The Bible tells us in Matthew 7:6, *"Do not give dogs what is sacred; do not throw your pearls to pigs."* Valuable things are not given to those not part of the fold. It is reserved for those who are a part of the body and have given their lives to Jesus. Acts 2:38 puts this into perspective for us.

Then Peter said to them, "Repent, and let every one of you be baptized in the name of Jesus Christ for the remission of sins; and you shall receive the gift of the Holy Spirit. For the promise is to you and to your children, and to all who are far off, as many as the Lord our God will call." (Acts 2:38)

Can you imagine a parent giving the same benefits, rights, and access to inheritance and precious jewels to a stranger on the side of the road as they would their children? I'm sure you can't even fathom that? So how much more our loving Father reserves the treasures of Heaven and its benefits for His children? Do you think that you must be perfect to access any of God's blessings? No, that is an illusion. What you do have to be, though, is to be born again. The Bible tells us in John 3:3, *"Except a man is born again, he cannot see the kingdom of God,"* and these valuable gifts are inside the kingdom of God. In Canada, there are certain benefits that you would not be entitled to unless you are a citizen or permanent resident. As a stopover tourist enroute to another country, you cannot say that you want to vote during your brief stopover in Canada during elections. In the same way, there is no way that an unbeliever or someone who has yet to be born again can be entitled to the things of those who have given and committed their lives to Christ? What benefit would it be to those born again if it were a free for all?

ALIGNMENT

To receive grace from God, you must be aligned with His will for your life, and in alignment with the authority he has placed over you, 2 Chronicles 20:20. When you go to a restaurant, the waiter is not the one that prepares the food. They make the food cooked by the chef available to you. If we use that same concept for the body of Christ, the Pastor is the waiter, and the chef is the Holy Spirit. You need to believe that the chef is skilled at cooking and believe that the waiter has your best interest at heart.

So they rose early in the morning and went out into the Wilderness of Tekoa; and as they went out, Jehoshaphat stood and said, "Hear me, O Judah and you inhabitants of Jerusalem: Believe in the Lord your God, and you shall be established; believe His prophets, and you shall prosper." (2 Chronicles 20:20)

Some people only believe in the chef but have no belief in the waiter serving the food to them, and therefore want to go into the kitchen to the chef themselves. But this is not the protocol. The bible tells us in Romans 8:28 that all things work together for good to those who love God. So, if we believe in God, we too must believe in His servants and messengers.

It makes logical sense to know that if your heavenly Father, who loves you so much, brought you here, you do not need to be defensive with the word or those He has sent to deliver the word. Settle down with the reassurance that your Father in Heaven loves you and receive the word. Can you imagine bringing gadgets to test the safety of the food every time your mom cooks for you? You wouldn't do this because you trust your mom and believe she won't knowingly or intentionally harm you. You know that you're safe. My mother makes some dishes that smell like food that's not to be eaten, but I know regardless of the aroma, it is safe for my consumption.

EARNESTLY DESIRE THE GIFT

You might be born again, aligned, but you may not have any desire for the gift. For example, as a student, you can decide to read every book, do research to write an assignment, or you can read as guided by the Holy Spirit and pass with distinction. This is my testimony. When my mother-in-law transitioned, I was enrolled in two courses. Four weeks later, my dad transitioned while I was still taking the same two courses. Fear came saying, "you better drop those courses," but I strengthened myself in God and told myself that He knew this would happen long before I started the classes, so I don't need to withdraw. I received 100% on one and 98% on the other, amid mourning and leading the CCCG movement. So, I am not talking about something far-fetched and theoretical. I'm talking about something I have applied and experienced. Yet, there are some that are not mourning over the transitioning of a loved one, are not pastoring, and their only focus is school, yet it's a struggle.

Challenge yourself in God. Earnestly desire the gifts He has made available in the body of Christ. You might be saying, "Lord, I don't want to struggle." Many people are in need because they don't know what they need. If you are spirit-filled, prove it by your results. Ask Him, "Lord, I don't want these kinds of results, what exactly am I lacking?" He will let you know the things you're lacking, and you'll fill in those blanks with what you desire.

When what you're saying makes sense, people will listen to you. Queen Sheba came all the way from Kush to hear the wisdom of Solomon (1 Kings 10). There was a time one of the wives came to me complaining that her husband doesn't go to her for advice. I responded by saying, "does what you have to say make sense? If yes, then your husband will listen to you. Instead of you using force, ask God for wisdom". Now her husband listens to her advice.

Don't fake something that can be real. It is not by age; it is by grace. I have not seen anybody that will go to the devil saying, "I am 60 years old I command you to leave" the devil will tell you he is not leaving because he has no age. It is not by how much a person has; it is by grace. Desire the grace and use the gifts of the spirit to continuously build yourself (1 Corinthians 12).

How will you know you have grace in a particular area? You'll see results. If you're yet to see the results, keep asking for grace. You see, faith is to help you get to a point where you can see it, you have it in your hands, then you don't need the faith for that anymore. You don't say you have wisdom by faith for ten years, and there are no results. The Bible says wisdom is demonstrated by her children, that is, by her works.

I used to struggle with my self-esteem until I saw myself. I heard a story of a lion that lost its company amongst the lions and went to grow up among sheep. The lion, alongside the sheep, would see other lions and run. One day, the lion went by a river to drink water. Looking in the water, the lion saw that it looked like the other lions it was running away from. So, the next time the lions came to attack, he went and crossed over to the other side instead of running. When I saw who God made me in the spirit, I stopped running.

I don't know what your desire is but according to where you know you are going to God, just begin to desire it.

Channels of Impartation

The Bible says the labour of fools wearies everyone, for they know not how to get to the city (Ecclesiastes 10:15). Many people know about the blessings and benefits of God's gifts, but not everybody knows how to receive them. When this is the case, you'll find people giving money to others to get the gift, like Simon, the sorcerer in the book of Acts. You'll also find people manipulating their way to get gifts, others losing their integrity and being taken advantage of to encounter grace. But why go through all this trouble when there is a more excellent way?

We need to correctly position ourselves before God to receive spiritual gifts. Paul said in Romans 1:11, *For I long to see you, that I may impart to you some spiritual gift, so that you may be established.* Impart means to transfer, to communicate from one person to another.

Paul made us understand in 1 Corinthians 15:10, which says, *but by the grace of God I am what I am,* that every single person is made by grace. Permit me to say, you can use faith to receive grace, but you don't need faith to know that you have grace. The grace of God is evident and tangible and must therefore be visible. How can you say by faith that you have the grace for diligence and yet have nothing to show for it? Now don't get me wrong, there is nothing wrong with that. It just means you need to keep trusting God until it comes. And when grace does indeed come, you will know without a shadow of a doubt. God has made all these things available, and He wants them to be your portion. I don't know what you have identified as your need but continue to have that desire.

Every gift God has made available is your right if you know how to get it. Of course, you can ask God for it, but there are ways these graces can be imparted into you. Some students think passing an exam is only by studying and attending classes. It's good to study, but not everybody that studies understand what they are studying. Go and ask the Ethiopian eunuch who was reading and reading, almost going bald until Philip came and explained it to him.

The channels of grace discussed in earlier chapters will show you how to build and maintain the grace that has been made available to you. This section on the impartation of grace is about how to tap into the grace that others have labored for. Jesus Christ confirmed that we can reap what others have labored to get. In John 4:38, Jesus said, *"I sent you to reap that for which you have not labored; others have labored, and you have entered into their labors."* How is this not different from stealing the harvest of others? The answer is that if God sends us to take steps that will lead to receiving from others' harvest, then that is not stealing.

Apostle Paul validated the possibility of tapping into the grace that others have laboured for when he said,

just as it is right for me to think this of you all, because I have you in my heart, inasmuch as both in my chains and in the defense and confirmation of the gospel, you all are partakers with me of grace. (Philippians 1:7)

In Ephesians 4:7-16, we also see that the five-fold offices are the container for the grace of God that came through Christ. (See more information about the five-fold offices in the book, Finding your Place: The Five-Fold Offices by Emmanuel Adewusi). Apostle Paul called each office "grace" in Ephesians 4:7. When Jesus rose from the dead, He gave gifts to everyone. Perhaps it's better to say, Jesus made everyone potentially a gift to everyone. What Jesus did on the cross and afterward meant that every human being, especially believers, carries something special that can enrich other peoples' lives. Are you a prophet, pastor, teacher, evangelist, or apostle? The five-fold office you occupy contains grace that every other office needs to be perfected.

The channels of grace will help you grow in the grace you already occupy. On the other hand, the impartation of grace will help you benefit from the grace that other people embody. Let's now dive right into the different ways grace can be imparted from one carrier of grace to another.

WORDS

Go ahead and tell me that course that you're not doing well in, and I can tell you that, to a certain degree you don't admire or honor the professor. How often have you taken notes when a loved one is telling you something? Hardly ever, right? But yet it is etched in your memory forever, and you'll always "remember it like yesterday" but didn't take notes. Why? Love. Love makes you pay attention to someone, retain what they've said, and give them direct access to your heart. The spirit doesn't have memory issues, it is only the human mind that struggles to remember.

We can receive the words when we walk in love and honor because it is a heart-to-heart connection. Some time ago, the Lord asked me if I knew why Joshua was strong. Do you know how many times God told Joshua "Be strong and of good courage"? God was not implying that he was weak. Every time God spoke those words, He was imparting strength to him. There are people I tell "be bold," and they think I am saying they are weak or lack confidence, but they don't understand. In saying those words, I was adding to what they already had. I tell them, "You need to be wise" and they get offended, yet it was an impartation of wisdom. No wonder Joshua was strong and bold, just winning one battle after another.

Words can be a channel of impartation of grace. John 6:63 says, *"The words that I speak to you are spirit, and they are life."* Do you see what Jesus was saying here? He didn't say the words I speak to everybody, but rather the words I speak to you. Jesus was specifically saying to you. When Elijah was about to be taken up, he asked Elisha what he wanted, and Elisha said he wanted a double portion of his spirit. Elijah said something very telling in response; he said if you see me taken up, then it's yours. There were 50 other prophets who were also looking at Elijah, so Elijah was talking about a different "see." So again, "the words I speak to you." Words can be spoken generally and often in crowds, such as in churches, but you will know which one is yours. This is how impartation begins to come.

And he said to me, "O Daniel, man greatly beloved, understand the words that I speak to you, and stand upright, for I have now been sent to you." While he was speaking this word to me, I stood trembling. (Daniel 10:11)

Sometimes, there is a visible reaction when that word of impartation is coming. There are times when I'm delivering a prophetic word to people, and they begin to cry and shake. Some were getting there and shut it down because they didn't have the understanding. Don't be carnally minded; allow the Holy Spirit to do His work in you. This is all a part of the impartation process. If you begin to cry, allow yourself to cry. Don't rob yourself by focusing on what people will say or think. Just focus on the experience and what is happening to you; otherwise, you'll disengage and come out of that experience and miss out.

And he said, "O man greatly beloved, fear not! Peace be to you; be strong, yes, be strong!" So when he spoke to me I was strengthened, and said, "Let my lord speak, for you have strengthened me." (Daniel 10:19)

The main thing here is the word. And it can be communicated through text, audible hearing, or seeing, so long as you receive it. Sometimes people send me long messages, and I reply, "It is well," and they are offended because they are looking for a philosopher or a comforter, but that is the Holy Spirit. If you receive it, you receive it. You don't need long messages filled with fluff. All you need are words of life regardless of the length of the reply. "You are perfected in Jesus' name. Receive wisdom in the name of Jesus". The beauty of this is that no matter how short the message, you've received your breakthrough if the Spirit of God backs it. Make sure you fill-up the same way you received the initial impartation. So, if you received words, keep filling up by hearing and meditating on words of life. We could liken it to something I once heard, if you needed a ladder to go up, you'd need a ladder to stay up.

Some people are like the five foolish virgins that left with no extra oil for their lamps, not knowing that the oil would finish. You keep enough words for the day. For some, it is only Sunday they hear the word of life. You can arrange your life in a way to receive words of life every day of the week, and suddenly you'll realize you're elevating.

Be mindful, however, as the words you hear can release grace but can also take grace from you. Psalms 1:1 says, *Blessed is the man Who walks not in the counsel (words) of the ungodly Nor stands in the path of sinners (so they won't hear the words of sinners), Nor sits in the seat of the scornful.*

The main tool of scornful people is words. Just as you ought to fill up in the same way you received grace, whichever way you receive grace is the same way grace can be taken from you. If the main channel of impartation that God has designed for you are words, you must be extra vigilant with the kind of words you give your ear and open your heart. God has told you what needs to be done, you must put aside everyone else's opinion. For example, God showed me the location of our church building and told me that was where we were going to be. Many things were happening to disprove His words, but I knew I couldn't give room to any of it because words are one of the ways that I receive impartation. If you're around complainers, you're likely experiencing a decline in grace because complaining short circuits the faith. This is why I'm quick to disconnect when I hear complaining. I take steps to ensure that nothing another person does hinders the grace of God in my life.

LAYING ON OF HANDS

One of the ways grace is imparted is by touch, which many know as laying on of hands. However, it must be intentional, both by the vessel and the recipient. The Bible says in Matthew 13:25 that "but while men slept, his enemy came and sowed tares among the wheat and went his way." It is only when the devil wants to destroy people that things come mistakenly. You may not have known, but when God blesses, it is intentional. It's not just by happenstance.

Now Joshua the son of Nun was full of the spirit of wisdom, for Moses had laid his hands on him; so the children of Israel heeded him, and did as the Lord had commanded Moses. (Deuteronomy 34:9)

The laying on of hands is a common way for grace upon one person to be transferred to another. In Acts 13:3, Paul (formerly Saul) and Barnabas were imparted with grace by the church leadership before they were sent off to ministry. I have had hands laid on me for the impartation of grace for ministry and I see that grace working day by day.

We went to a particular conference when I was a new youth Pastor, someone asked a question, and I began to say things I did not know before. People were expecting foolishness, but they began to hear wisdom. This was when I began to understand the prayer the Pastor told me to pray. Let God validate your leadership, and one of the ways is through the laying on of hands. With intention, you know what you're getting. I used to love to sleep because I was bullied, so sleeping was my safe space, but when grace came, the desire for sleep just left. Joshua also experienced the grace for honor and authority when Moses laid his hands on him with that intention in mind.

And the Lord said to Moses: "Take Joshua the son of Nun with you, a man in whom is the Spirit, and lay your hand on him; set him before Eleazar the priest and before all the congregation, and inaugurate him in their sight. And you shall give some of your authority to him, that all the congregation of the children of Israel may be obedient. (Numbers 27:18-20)

Have you had hands laid on you for the purpose of an impartation of grace? Now, I am challenging you to allow that grace to flow. You don't need to feel the effect. Instead, begin to demonstrate the work that needs to validate your faith. Once hands have been laid on you by a carrier of grace, believe you have received your desire. Apostle Paul challenged Timothy to allow the grace he has received to manifest in 2 Timothy 1:6.

Therefore I remind you to stir up the gift of God which is in you through the laying on of my hands. You don't have to feel anything when hands are laid on you, just have faith.

If you have never had hands laid on you, I encourage you to prayerfully seek a spiritual leader that can lay hands to bless you. You don't have to look for some random person to lay hands on you. If you have parents or even a pastor, make every effort to get them to lay hands on your head to bless you.

ANOINTED MATERIALS (MANTLES)

One of the earliest mentions of a mantle for the transfer of power is found in the life of the Prophet Elijah. A mantle is any item that an anointed person uses. It could be a clothing item, a technological device, a chair, etc. In Elijah's case, the mantle was his cloak.

Now Elijah took his mantle, rolled it up, and struck the water; and it was divided this way and that, so that the two of them crossed over on dry ground. And so it was, when they had crossed over, that Elijah said to Elisha, "Ask! What may I do for you, before I am taken away from you? Elisha said, "Please let a double portion of your spirit be upon me." (2 Kings 2:8-9)

Elisha understood that there was something different about Elijah. You see, you cannot receive value if you don't see the value. You can be in a miracle while still looking for miracles. Elisha saw value in Elijah, which enabled him to request for the virtues he saw in Elijah. 2 Kings 2:10 stated Elijah's response to Elisha's request, *"You have asked a hard thing. Nevertheless, if you see me when I am taken from you, it shall be so for you; but if not, it shall not be so."*

One of the reasons why some people fail to receive impartation or the transference of giftings is because of a competitive spirit. They don't want to see others lifted in their presence, and some even compete with their spiritual and biological parents, mentors, etc. But look at what Elijah said, if you are present and you see me being elevated before your very eyes, you'll be elevated. You can't get it until I am elevated. This means one of the prayers we ought to pray is to ask the Lord to keep blessing and elevating our mentors. So, when the enemy tempts you to compete with your superiors, he is trying to keep you stagnant. When you wake up after receiving a dream of someone being elevated, how do you respond? Do you wake up excited, or do you wake up and say, God, what about me? Your response is of utmost importance because this is God testing your heart.

Then it happened, as they continued on and talked, that suddenly a chariot of fire appeared with horses of fire, and separated the two of them; and Elijah went up by a whirlwind into heaven. And Elisha saw it, and he cried out, "My father, my father, the chariot of Israel and its horsemen!" So he saw him no more. And he took hold of his own clothes and tore them into two pieces. He also took up the mantle of Elijah that had fallen from him, and went back and stood by the bank of the Jordan. Then he took the mantle of Elijah that had fallen from him, and struck the water, and said, "Where is the Lord God of Elijah?" And when he also had struck the water, it was divided this way and that; and Elisha crossed over. (2 Kings 2:11-14)

The double portion came upon Elisha through the item he took that belonged to Elijah, known as a mantle. But he didn't take it; it was given to him. There is a mystery about the transference of grace through materials. Many people misuse this, but again, any good thing can be counterfeited. The fact that some irresponsible people operate as counterfeits does not mean that the action itself is not valid. In Acts 19, clothes were taken from the body of Paul, and there was power in it that moved from one person to another, which further confirms that the anointing can be transferred through materials. It is high time that the body of Christ grows in that revelation.

It is very interesting how many people only understand the demonic aspect of it. If someone says a cloth came from a shrine and incantations were done on it, many people will not collect it because they know that the cloth isn't ordinary, and it possesses the power to bring about an unideal reality. In their mind, the power in the cloth from the occultist is more than a mantle from God-ordained men or women.

You may still be wondering 'how does this all work, in theory?" The presence of God is a tangible item, which is why, when people are touched, they feel something tangible. The grace of God is tangible, and it can be captured and transferred. That's why the woman with the issue of blood knew she didn't need to speak to talk to Jesus or have him speak to her or lay hands. She knew just touching Him or anything within His vicinity would bring about her healing. The grace of God knows no borders and can be accessed even through material items.

From Apostle Peter's example in Acts 5:15, even a shadow can become a mantle. Don't limit yourself to the common opportunities for the impartation of grace. Our mind is the only hindrance to how far the concept of the mantle can be applied. Once you know that the individual is a carrier of the grace you desire, your faith will determine what a mantle can be to you. The Holy Spirit is the one that will choose what spiritual gift will be distributed and the means of distribution (1 Corinthians 12:11).

SERVICE

Serving is another way to connect with the grace of God at work. I heard a story of a Pastor who noticed that children of anointed servants of God were going astray and wondered if it was the devil. This pastor had a hard time believing that children of anointed men and women of God could go astray because of the proximity to the anointing. He discovered that one of the reasons was that although they were close to the anointing, they were not partaking in the anointing. He then decided to make sure that his children served him directly when he was in church.

Some people think because of who their mother and father are, that good things will be automatic in life. In the previous section, we spoke about how Elisha received a double portion of Elijah. We didn't discuss how he received the double portion through service even before asking for it. You see, you can do something right but not understand what you're doing; therefore, you won't get the best results. But once you begin to understand your actions, you'll begin to get the best results. Let's look at Elisha's secret that qualified him for Elijah's anointing.

But Jehoshaphat said, "Is there no prophet of the Lord here, that we may inquire of the Lord by him? "So one of the servants of the king of Israel answered and said, "Elisha the son of Shaphat is here, who poured water on the hands of Elijah" (2 Kings 3:11).

Elisha was entitled to the grace of God upon Elijah because of his dedicated service. Can you imagine someone managing the finances of a millionaire and still be a pauper? Or can you imagine someone being an administrator of a billionaire's estate and yet be homeless? It is practically impossible. Serving someone carrying the grace of God you desire will make you a candidate for that grace. It is important to serve the carrier of God's grace who is also an authority over you with a good understanding of the realm it can open you up to.

We can tap into the grace of God by serving both God and His anointed. Elisha had access because he poured water on the hands of Elijah. There were many prophets there, but the Bible never said they poured water on the hands of Elijah.

One of the biggest hindrances to this way of impartation is pride. The Bible tells us something in James 4:6, *'But He gives more grace. Therefore, he says: "God resists the proud, but gives grace to the humble."* By positioning yourself in humility, God can give you things you didn't even ask for. I have yet to see a person who will go to their workplace and ask the supervisor's age because they don't serve people younger than them. I don't see it happening in the workplace but see so much of it in the body of Christ. That is the epitome of pride at work. People can drop their ego when going to work and then pick it back up when they go to church, yet the church is way more reputable and honourable than any other institution.

James 4:10 says, *"Humble yourselves in the sight of the Lord, and He will lift you up."* Where is the sight of the Lord? Everywhere. Humble yourself in your home because that is the sight of the Lord. Humble yourself in the workplace because that is also the sight of the Lord. How will He lift you up? By giving you grace. Over time, I realized Elisha could have gone to God and asked for grace, but God would have directed him right back to Elijah. In fact, that is what God has done for many people, but they have refused to be redirected.

When we see people getting results in an area that we are struggling with, we need to learn to humble ourselves and ask them what they are doing right and what we are lacking that they have. This is how we can grow in knowledge, wisdom, and grace. When we add what we receive from someone to what we already have, we will move higher if only we humble ourselves. Nobody is saying you don't have grace, but the amount of grace that you can continue to receive is unending. God has great things for you that are your right if only you ask for it. You need to be humble enough to know what you don't have. That is one of the ways you define humility, having an accurate picture of your strengths and weaknesses. That is why proud people run themselves to the ground because they can never admit their mistakes and see themselves as superhumans. But a humble person, even with a knowledge of faith, will know their limitations.

No wonder the Bible said Moses was the meekest on all the earth. He knew his limitation was in his speech. So, you need to identify what you don't have and locate where it is, then begin to serve with an understanding of what you're doing. For example, you can pray, "Father at this moment I've realized I don't have wisdom in relationships.

Lord, I need that wisdom". So now, as you're serving God and the one that carries the grace you desire, you're trusting God for relationship wisdom. This is the key point here. In short, without humility, it is impossible to serve God or his anointed.

Let's zoom into Joshua. We know he was full of wisdom because Moses laid his hands on him, as we saw in the book of Deuteronomy. The book of Numbers comes before Deuteronomy, so let's see what God said before Moses laid hands on him.

For in the Wilderness of Zin, during the strife of the congregation, you rebelled against My command to hallow Me at the waters before their eyes." (These are the waters of Meribah, at Kadesh in the Wilderness of Zin.) Then Moses spoke to the Lord, saying: "Let the Lord, the God of the spirits of all flesh, set a man over the congregation, who may go out before them and go in before them, who may lead them out and bring them in, that the congregation of the Lord may not be like sheep which have no shepherd." And the Lord said to Moses: "Take Joshua the son of Nun with you, a man in whom is the Spirit, and lay your hand on him" (Numbers 27:14-18)

As you can see, even before Moses laid hands on him, the Spirit of God was already inside of him. How did the spirit get there? Through service, wisdom is followed by the laying on of hands. There are different graces we desire, and there are many ways God can choose to impart that grace into our lives.

Every time Moses went up to the mountain, Joshua trailed behind. Moses stayed there, and Joshua remained there also. Joshua served with all of himself, not with eyeservice. He was jealousy serving to the point where he saw people prophesying, knowing it was supposed to be Moses' job. He went to Moses, telling him he wanted to shut them down, but Moses instructed him to leave them alone as he wanted more prophets in Israel. So, Joshua was all in.

Let me define service. Service is not just doing something but meeting a need that exists. Many people are doing many things but are not actually serving because what they are doing is not adding value to anybody.

You know to ask questions if you are doing what they told you to do but continuously not seeing results. What you are doing must add value. When you add so much value that it touches the heart of God or the person you're serving, there is a release.

In 2 Samuel 23, David longed for water from Bethlehem; this was a need. The people around him were aware that it was a point of impartation, so they went to the extent of killing people to get the water. Now, I'm not saying to go and kill anyone in the name of serving and meeting a need. I am simply illustrating the dedication of service. Many people are doing tasks in their workplace that are not even needed, sending reports or requests nobody reads. Some of them bring these same actions into the house of God. Service is meeting a need that exists. Service is also timely. That water they gave David at that time was more valuable than ten luxury vehicles because he already had so many of them.

I encountered a highly-sought-after servant of God many years ago and was privileged to have lunch with him after the church service. I was seated next to him when the Holy Spirit inspired me to ask him if he had written a book. He said no but that he had desired to write a book for many, many years. The Holy Spirit had laid it on my heart to give him one of the books I authored. I then offered to assist him with his book which he gladly accepted. My ability to meet the specific need he had distinguished me from everyone else, including someone who might have given him thousands of dollars. I now have direct access to him, and it is a relationship I cherish very much.

It takes the wisdom of God to see a need and the grace of God to meet the need. Hardly will anyone forget the one who helped them in their time of need. One of the things I've realized is that one of the ways God blesses people is by opening their eyes to see a need in the life of someone else. Allow God to open your eyes; that is how Joshua got the anointing upon Moses, which prepared him to receive the wisdom he needed.

Let me tell you something, the devil always waits for people at the point of their blessings, not at any useless place. God has opened your eyes, then fear begins to come, "oh if you do this then, and they don't do anything."

Imagine you didn't know Bill Gates but saw him stranded at a service station wanting to pay for gas, but his wallet was stolen. You just happened to be around to pay for $60 worth of gas for him. That $60 would have way more value than gifting him one million dollars after being stranded.

Some of us need to ask God for forgiveness because He opened our eyes to see needs, but we were nonchalant, lazy, or rationalized it, causing someone else to step in. These are practical things that we can do to position ourselves for impartation, and then suddenly, you'll see that you are growing in grace and the things you couldn't do before you're now doing with ease.

Begin to ask yourself if what you are doing is adding value. Is it needed? Is it meeting a need, or are you just doing something that needs to be done? I can tell you that if you begin to meet needs, you'll never lack grace.

GIVING

Many people are aware of the negative impartation of giving but are completely unaware of the positive impartation of giving. What do

I mean by the negative impartation of giving? Some demonic people ask for money not because they want to use it for something good but for evil. Money is a means of exchange when done intentionally. You can't go to the store, see the price of an item, and throw the money in the air, then walk away with the item. They'll call the police. It's an intentional transaction with intentional actions. You know what you want, you know what it costs, and you pay the price for it.

Someone said man's greatest need is that man doesn't know what they need. They have a need, but they don't know what they need. Giving is another way to get the grace you desire. This is how Solomon received wisdom. I still hear people today saying that even after three years with no progress, they still trust God. They fail to understand that they're not going about things the right way. They will eventually begin to blame God and become cynical in their walk, especially when seeing Him answering the prayers of others. Don't be stubborn in your heart. If what you're doing is right, why are we not seeing the results? You receive grace by faith, but you don't need faith to operate in grace because we can see when grace is at work. Solomon did not operate in wisdom by faith. We saw the wisdom operating. Let's look at what Solomon did,

And Solomon loved the Lord, walking in the statutes of his father David, except that he sacrificed and burned incense at the high places. 4 Now the king went to Gibeon to sacrifice there, for that was the great high place: Solomon offered a thousand burnt offerings on that altar. (1 Kings 3:3-4)

Let me tell you something, the Bible didn't say this, but you can use one scripture to interpret another scripture. When Solomon was giving his offering, he already knew that he wanted wisdom. His father gave him certain marching orders before he passed, one of which was to lead the people with wisdom. Why do I say that? Let's look at verse 5, *At Gibeon the Lord appeared to Solomon in a dream by night; and God said, "Ask! What shall I give you?"* How will you know he truly had this in his heart in real life? Because it was there even in the dream.

The gift of God is not for sale; it cannot be bought with money or service. Simon, the sorcerer, took the money and gave it to Peter, wanting what he had, but Peter said to him "your money perishes with you." But like in the case of Solomon, it is not you paying for it when God Himself told you what to do. I remember going to a conference in the U.S.A, and the Holy Spirit told me to give all the money in my pocket to the pastor leading the prayer. As he was praying, I took the money out, put it in an envelope, gave it to him, and left. That same man is my spiritual father today. This was at a time when I was asking God, "Lord you're bringing people you want me to father, but who is going to father me?" I knew the three persons He had put in authority over the ministry, but I didn't have access to them yet. And you must have access to a person you say is fathering you. Many people sit at home watching different Pastors and don't have a connection with any of them. And as a result, we have many Christians being damaged by the enemy today because they have no one to reach out to when going through challenges.

The elevation and growth resulting from following that instruction from the Holy Spirit have been mind-boggling. I didn't go there with money because I wanted a connection. In fact, I wasn't even aware that I would receive that instruction until that very moment. A person who is aware of and values the grace they have will not collect money in that manner because, again, the gift is not for sale.

2 Corinthians 8 shows us there is grace when it comes to giving. It reads, *Moreover, brethren, we make known to you the grace of God bestowed on the churches of Macedonia: that in a great trial of affliction, the abundance of their joy and their deep poverty abounded in the riches of their liberality. For I bear witness that according to their ability, yes, and beyond their ability,*

they were freely willing, imploring us with much urgency that we would receive the gift and the fellowship of the ministering to the saints. We all have needs and desires, so when you see a person giving beyond their ability, without being put under pressure or recognized for their giving, yet they are consistent, know that grace is at work.

It truly takes the grace of God to give even when you're not recognized for your giving. Many people love to receive recognition and praise for their giving. A person who gave $30,000 in donations might compare themselves to someone who gave $5.00 and believes that their own was more sacrificial. This kind of thinking is completely wrong because many fail to realize that when a person gives to God, God judges the state of each person's heart and knows the capacity from which each person gave. The one who gave $5.00 can appear more pleasing and acceptable in God's eyes because they took from what they had and did not hold back on God. Whereas the one who gave $30,000 may not be acceptable to God because from the abundance they have been given, $30,000 is no match.

Master Keys to any Grace you Desire

What if you want all the things we have mentioned? What do you do? You need to trust God for the ability to love and honour anybody and anything, even a little child. With love and honour in your toolbox, you can have access to any grace available on the face of the earth. David had this grace. He saw the Amalekite that was near death, and he gave him food in a dignified manner, and he enjoyed the grace that the man carried in the face of death.

You see, every good thing is locked up somewhere. That is why the Bible says in Isaiah 45:3, *'I will give you the treasures of darkness and hidden riches of secret places, that you may know that I, the Lord, who call you by your name, Am the God of Israel.'* You see grace at work, but you may not see or understand how to get there unless God opens your eyes. Love and honor open the door to spiritual things. The Bible says the heart of man is very deep, but love and honor opens the door. Everything we have talked up to this point is a demonstration of love and honour.

1 Corinthians 12:31 says, *but earnestly desire the best gifts. And yet I show you a more excellent way*, then chapter 13 goes on to talk about love. When you begin to get close to a servant of God, one of the things you'll fight is offense, some of it will make sense, and some of it will absolutely make no sense at all, but you'll still feel it. The enemy wants to short-circuit your ability to connect with what you need to get.

Then He went out from there and came to His own country, and His disciples followed Him. And when the Sabbath had come, He began to teach in the synagogue. And many hearing Him were astonished, saying, "Where did this Man get these things? And what wisdom is this which is given to Him, that such mighty works are performed by His hands!" So they identified that this man carries gifts, He is not where He is by His own grace, but then they descended into dishonor and got offended in the next verse. *"Is this not the carpenter, the Son of Mary, and brother of James, Joses, Judas, and Simon? And aren't His sisters here with us?" So they were offended at Him.* (Mark 6:1-3)

So you can see here that love and honour were missing. Jesus went on to say,

But Jesus said to them, "A prophet is not without honor except in his own country, among his own relatives, and in his own house." Now He could do no mighty work there, except that He laid His hands on a few sick people and healed them. (Mark 6:4-5)

Honour triggers the prophetic grace and every other grace. The place where people need to be careful the most is in the vicinity of the anointing of God. Jesus said that if there was honour, the prophetic grace will move in ways they won't even imagine. The anointing wasn't flowing for Him to even heal them.

So how do we keep tapping into grace until Jesus comes? Love and honour. When you see someone moving forward, duplicating the grace of God, this is the secret. Don't be part of those involved in eyeservice, pretending in the front but mocking in the back.

When people share testimonies, you can meet with them and ask for more details. What steps did you take? What did you do to get there? Nobody is a superstar; they are simply people that God is helping. I cannot pray enough. I cannot fast enough or pray all the prayers I'll ever pray. One way or another, there will be a deficiency. I do my best, and I live with that deficiency, knowing His grace will make up for the difference. The Bible says that when you are weak, I will make you strong.

Walking in love and honour will get you to the point where you can connect with any grace you desire regardless of whether they are dead or alive. Moses fasted for 40 days twice, but you will never read in the Bible that Joshua fasted. Yet, Joshua did what Moses did not get to do; Joshua led the Israelites into the promised land. Oftentimes, people run off too fast and pray to receive an anointing without first asking the Holy Spirit how to go about receiving the gift. 1 Corinthians 12 ended with the direction to seek a more excellent way to connect with spiritual gifts. That more excellent way is the way of love!

5

Evidence of Connection

Now that we have explored the different channels through which you can seamlessly connect with God, how would you know when you've made that connection with God? You would know you've made a genuine connection to God through your body, soul, and spirit.

Man is made up of spirit, soul, and body (1 Thessalonians 5:23). The soul is made up of the will, the mind, and emotions. When you connect with God, it can touch different aspects of your being. It can touch your emotions and give you overwhelming joy or tears. It can affect you mentally, where your mind was racing and is now peaceful. Sometimes it can impact your body, causing shaking, trembling, and fluctuations in temperature. Does that happen all at once or with the same intensity? No, it does not. However, every time we connect with God, it touches at least one aspect of our being in varying degrees of intensity, depending on what God wants to do at that moment.

In this New Testament era, it is grace that we are enjoying. Jesus has died on the cross for you and I and has opened the doors to access every good thing in God. There is a way that seems right unto a man, but the ends are the ends of death. This means there are other ways that lead to life, not death. As we follow those ways, we begin to enjoy things other people are not enjoying, and one of the blessings that comes with it is speed.

Body

Paying attention to your bodily responses is important for more than just knowing when you've eaten some bad seafood. The way your body responds to being in the presence of God can be an indication of when you've connected with God. You can feel the presence of God through shaking or even a feeling of electricity going through your body. You must understand that you will not always feel the presence of God; otherwise, you can fall into the trap of discouragement. Some people think all they will need to hear is a word, but at the time, you will only feel the presence of God. There are times you'll be unable to stand because of the weight on you that the Bible refers to as the weight of glory. You feel heavy, in a good way, and suddenly feel the need to kneel or lie down, to be in a posture of submission before God.

An example of the effect of connecting with God on our bodies is what happened when Solomon was blessing the newly built sanctuary. The bible narrates that the glory of God was so strong that nobody could stay standing.

And it came to pass, when the priests came out of the holy place, that the cloud filled the house of the Lord, so that the priests could not continue ministering because of the cloud; for the glory of the Lord filled the house of the Lord. (1 Kings 8:10-11)

Soul

As mentioned earlier, the soul is composed of the will, mind, and emotions. Beginning with the will under the soul, In Luke 22, Jesus was praying, *"Lord let this cup pass over me but nevertheless not My will, but*

Your will be done." He kept praying and got to a point where He connected with grace. Do you know what it's like knowing you're going to die and preparing yourself to be killed? It is only the grace of God that can carry a person through that kind of ordeal. Once you connect to grace, you'll see yourself in Esther with the mindset of *"if I perish, I perish!"* You will begin to do what you couldn't do before.

Now, the mind. The mind is where many people focus their attention. How do you know you are connected? When God begins to speak, your mind can become fruitful. He can ask you a question or drop something in your spirit. I've found that many times He asks questions. There are times when, during worship, you suddenly hear, "what is your name?" It's not a trick question or your mind deceiving you. You may wonder what kind of question it is, but answer, and you've just received an encounter. I've also found that we value those falling experiences more than hearing.

When it comes to emotions, we can sometimes just begin to cry uncontrollably or even laugh. This happened a lot in Kenneth E Hagin's meetings. The presence of God would manifest so tangibly in these places that it would lead to bursts of laughter in the spirit.

Spirit

Anything that does not fall under the other categories falls under the spirit. There is so much in the spiritual realm that it cannot be exhaustively explained. For example, how can you explain an experience of you worshiping God then suddenly you are caught in a trance and no longer there? The Holy Ghost can take hold of your spirit and take it to wherever He wants once you have connected. People can see someone worshiping with their hands in the air and mouth moving, yet still, they are no longer there. Or how do you explain an experience where God appeared while you were eating, began to eat with you, and one piece of meat was missing? How will you explain that? To a carnally minded person, it will be a difficult concept to grasp. There are times when the Holy Spirit will forbid you from saying anything because sometimes, even a deeply spiritual person can find it difficult to understand.

Results

The grace of God will cause you to transition from operating as a human to operating as a divine personality. When the grace of God comes upon you, you will find yourself doing things you never thought you could do. An example was when Apostle Peter walked on water. You can say that Peter encountered the grace of God which made him operate beyond the realm of humans. In Matthew 14:28-29, we see that Peter operated by grace for a few minutes before coming back into the natural realm.

Regardless of whether you encountered the grace directly from God or through a carrier of grace, you will not remain the same after grace has been received. Just like physical healing, the moment the grace you are seeking has come upon you, the aspect of your being that needs the grace will begin to operate supernaturally for as long as you are leaning on the grace.

In Apostle Peter's walking on water example, the channel of grace was the word. The moment Peter received and acted on the word; he began to replicate the actions of the carrier of grace. The moment, however, that Peter took his mind off the source of grace, the grace was lost. I cannot help but wonder what would have happened if Peter didn't take his eyes off Jesus.

In many instances, you will not have a sensual response to the grace of God that has come upon you. The only way you will know that grace has been released is from the results you begin to generate. The bible did not record that Jacob fell under the anointing when his father, Isaac was blessing him. We, however, see the clear effect of that blessing upon Jacob as he began to amass wealth at an unprecedented pace. The most important evidence of grace should be in the result you generate. Keep your eyes fixed on your results as the pointer to whether you have been touched by God or not.

Epilogue

I pray that every one of us is confident, without doubt, in the place that we fit in. You know, especially when you're feeling tired or frustrated. Don't wait until you are frustrated to have this revelation. In case you didn't realize it and are already frustrated, your first response should no longer be to pray, "Oh God, give me grace. Give me grace. Give me grace."

Identify your primary channel of grace and let that be the default you go to first. For many of us, there are some outfits that we are drawn to by default. There are people that we learn to recognize by their outfits. There is no way you will see them for two weeks, and you won't see that outfit being repeated. It's almost as if it's their uniform. And it's not because they don't have many outfits, but because they have a connection to that one. This is the same with the channels of grace. While there are several channels, there is one that each of us, by default, connects to naturally and seamlessly. Apple allows us to reset the iPhone back to the default setting; in the same way, if ever you find yourself frustrated, go back, and reset through your default channel of grace.

With these channels of grace, there is quantity, and there is quality. There is a certain point that you'll get to within that channel that you'll recognize as the sweet spot, where you begin to get results. At the beginning of this book, we talked about things to avoid that can choke the grace of God. So, there must be a synergy between quantity and quality because it is at this intersection where they meet that we begin to hear the voice. What do I mean by quantity? This is the amount of time we dedicate to a particular thing, and in this case, it is the amount of time we spend in our channel of grace. There are different levels of a flattened tire, and sometimes we allow it to become so deflated before attending to it that we must pump air into it for a longer period before we begin to see it inflate. And what is quality? This has to do with the caliber of the content. Someone said to me that she never feels full when she eats junk food. The operative word here is "junk," and there is a reason why it is called this. You can't expect to be adequately filled by consuming something referred to as junk, so of course, your body will tell you that you need more food. And it should be better quality food. You see how consuming something of lesser quality (aka junk) causes us to go back for seconds, and maybe even more, yet when consuming something that is filling (aka quality), one time is sufficient. Why do something twice that can be done right the first time?

Therefore, as a result of us ignoring flat tires or consuming junk food, as it were, we can no longer survive on quick fixes. Instead, what we need is a retreat. And a retreat is simply an extended devotional time. Just as doctors can put us on bed rest for neglecting or overworking our body, in the same way, when we neglect daily top-ups that our spirit needs, we must go on spiritual bed rest. Not every retreat or spiritual bed rest is caused by neglect. There are times when based on the completed assignment or the one ahead, we must either recharge from the past or prepare for what's to come.

The Bible tells us about a group of people who served God with their lips, but their hearts were far from Him. No matter how easy something might be – even if it's your primary channel – if your heart is not in it, forget it because it would all be for naught! God sees the heart. You can be chatting with someone in a supposed heart-to-heart conversation yet distracted on Facebook. It's not the best. We all know what it's like when talking to someone and know they're not paying attention. How can you claim to be connecting with God, and you're distracted doing other things? I'm not saying you can't multitask, such as doing chores, while connecting with God, but it is a matter of the heart. Is your heart fully connected, or are there lingering distractions? Connecting with God is not difficult. He is our father, and His throne is called the throne of grace. Grace can be translated as ease, smoothness, or naturalness. So why would connecting to the ultimate throne of grace be a difficult feat? Once we connect with God, grace is released in abundance. So, our focus should therefore be "how can I connect with God?"

I've said previously that my main channel of grace is meditation. When I wake up in the morning, before I begin to pray, I go to my quiet room and immediately begin to meditate on the goodness of God, the word, or His acts. It becomes so overwhelming, and this is when I know I've connected with God. From there, I may go into prayer or sometimes the Word, and it's fun!

There is no rigidity when it comes to God, as that would be going back to the Old Testament. Paul called out the Galatian church for their foolishness of starting in the spirit but ending in carnality. We start powerfully in the move of God, and then we put together rigid and unscriptural parameters, and now it becomes a routine - "start with worship, then go to praise. From there, it's prayer time, then go to the Word, round up with another prayer, and then you're done." Some people continue with these types of routines for so long that before they even realize what's happening, they don't even know who God is anymore because all they were doing was fulfilling all righteousness.

We're not celebrating the means (channels of grace); rather, we're celebrating the end which is connecting with God. If you say you've been doing devotions every day and you have no inclination of whether you've connected with God or not, you need to stop and re-evaluate your ways. It's not enough to say, "I've been doing this for 25 years." What do you have to show for it? Or is it a case of being a "know it all like the Pharisees?" Nicodemus was different from the other Pharisees who pretended to know everything. When he connected with Christ, he asked how he could be saved. He thought, "I've seen a difference in the message of Christianity and I'm ready to adjust my ways.", and Jesus saw the sincerity in his heart. (John 3:1-21)

Jesus came not to take us back to the Old Testament, but it was a ministry of reconciliation to the Father. We have it better than Adam in the garden because he did not have the Holy Spirit inside of him. We can be connected with God throughout the day and take His presence with us wherever we go as Christians if we know what to do.

Our channel of grace is like connecting with God through speed-dial. If anybody tells you that connecting with God is extremely difficult, they are deceiving you, or they don't know what they are talking about. How many parents require their children to jump through all sorts of hoops before they can come to them? If that's the case for you, you need prayer! But our God is a loving father and does not impose such stringent and difficult requirements on us to connect with Him.

This is why it is important to identify your own channel of grace. But now, what do you do once you've identified it? You structure and build your devotional life around it. If, for example, I have an hour to do devotions, and I know that my main channel of grace is meditation, after I've prayed and worshiped God, most of my time will be spent meditating. My goal for my devotion is to connect with God to receive the strength I need for the day. We don't prepare to fight on the day of battle; we prepare before the battle.

There was a time I was preparing to preach in a different church, and since the topic was on praise, I decided to practice the day before in my room by dancing. While dancing, I bent down and got to a point where I froze and couldn't stand up because of the sudden yet excruciating back pain. Instantly, Colossians 2:15 just came up powerfully from inside of me: "Having disarmed principalities and powers, He made a public spectacle of them, triumphing over them in it." and I said, "Satan, get your hands off my back, now, in the name of Jesus," and immediately it was gone! In those few seconds, different thoughts, such as calling 911 and how I would no longer be able to preach, came to my mind, but I didn't allow those thoughts to remain. By the grace of God, I was strong when my day of battle came, and I prevailed!

What afflictions have you faced in the past that could have ended from its very beginning if you had enough grace to fight back? The key is to continuously build strength, always stay neck-deep in God and confidently know that He is God. Be still and know that the Lord of heaven's armies is by your side (Psalm 46:10). The affliction may intensify over time, but remain steadfast, standing firm in the grace that God gives you.

Is there any channel that is better than the other? No, they are all created equal to cater to people's different needs and makeup. Think of it as a group of friends agreeing to meet at the food court in a mall. They all live in different parts of town and will enter the mall through the entrance closest to them. But the goal is still to meet at the food court, regardless of which entrance they use. No entrance was better than the other; it was a matter of which one worked best for each one of them. The goal is to access the presence of God, and regardless of the access point (channel), once you access the presence, that is all that matters.

Imagine trying to ride a bike to Calgary. Now imagine yourself driving to Calgary. Better still, imagine you being driven by somebody else to Calgary. Even better than that is imagining yourself flying to Calgary. Most people will choose flying from these modes of transportation because of the minimal time required to travel. But when there is pride, you'll say no, I'll ride my bicycle. I don't want anybody to say it's because of them I got here. You'll get there after many people have achieved many things.

It's not about doing something once and then falling back for three months. You'll see yourself naturally duplicating the grace steps at a time because everyone is at a different stage in their walk with God. Nonetheless, you're still seeing it work for you which is my heart's desire for everybody.

It's like learning how to dress up. At one point, you're nude, and at the next point, you're dressed up. A time is coming when it will be difficult to survive without knowing God. We will all need to have a competitive advantage over artificial intelligence. The Holy Spirit should be able to tell you to "go here... go there... don't invest here... Don't invest there."

I pray you no longer have doubt as to where you fit in and that every one of us will enjoy the grace of God. Your default should no longer be "God give me grace; God give me grace." Know your primary channel of grace and let that be your default. One final thing to note, when you properly mix quantity with quality, you'll have lasting results. Quantity is the amount of time we dedicate to that thing. There are times when we've allowed our tire to deflate so much that we must pump it for a time before we begin to see the effect of the air. Something can be working, but because of how far we have gone in the opposite direction and how much we need, we may not see its effect until a while. I long to see you so that I may impart to you spiritual gifts. It will all make the difference between being given fish and being taught how to fish. May the Lord give you the grace to practice what you have learned and build a system around it.

Contact the Author

I know without a doubt that this book has been a blessing to you. I am looking forward to hearing your testimony.

You can contact me through email at emmanuel.adewusi@cc-cghq.org or visit www.emmanueladewusi.org for more information.

A Sinner's Prayer

Dear Heavenly Father,

I come to You in the Name of Jesus Christ.

You said in Your Word, "*Whosoever shall call upon the name of the Lord shall be saved*" (Romans 10:13). I am calling on Your Name, so I know you have saved me now.

You also said *that if you confess with your mouth the Lord Jesus and believe in your heart that God has raised Him from the dead, you will be saved. For with the heart one believes unto righteousness, and with the mouth, confession is made unto salvation* (Romans 10:9-10). I believe in my heart Jesus Christ is the Son of God. I believe that He was raised from the dead for my justification, and I confess Him now as my Lord and Savior.

Thank you, Lord, because now, I am saved!

Thank You, Lord, because I know you have heard my prayer. Thank You, Lord, because I am now born again.

Signed _____

Date _____

Emmanuel Adewusi is the Founding and Lead Pastor of Cornerstone Christian Church of God.

Called into ministry with the mandate to "bring restoration and transformation to all by teaching, preaching and demonstrating the gospel of Jesus Christ," he is passionate to see lives restored and transformed the way God intended from the beginning of creation. He has a passion for the full counsel of the word of God, fellowship with the Holy Spirit and being under spiritual authority.

He hosts several *"Come and See"* Conferences, with the goal to reach lost souls for Jesus Christ.

He authored the books *"Now That You Are Born Again, What Next?"*, *"The Blessings of Being Under Spiritual Authority,"* *"A Disciplined Life,"* *"Interconnected Systems: A Wisdom Manual,"* and other impactful titles. He has also released an album titled *"Divine Encounter"* and many more on the way.

Emmanuel Adewusi is joyfully married to his wife, Ibukun Adewusi, and together, they are building a thriving Christ-centered family.

www.ingramcontent.com/pod-product-compliance
Lightning Source LLC
Chambersburg PA
CBHW070331010526
44107CB00004B/495